UNDER THE KNIFE

Life Lessons from the Operating Theatre

Liz O'Riordan

unbound

First published in 2023

Unbound
c/o TC Group, 6th Floor King's House, 9–10 Haymarket, London SW1Y 4BP
www.unbound.com
All rights reserved

This book is a work of non-fiction based on the life, experiences and
recollections of Liz O'Riordan. In some cases names of people, places, dates,
sequences or the detail of events have been changed solely to protect the privacy
of others. The author has stated to the publishers that, except in such minor
respects not affecting the substantial accuracy of the work,
the contents of this book are true.

Text design by Jouve

A CIP record for this book is available from the British Library

ISBN 978-1-80018-241-7 (paperback)
ISBN 978-1-80018-242-4 (ebook)

Printed in Great Britain by Clays Ltd, Elcograf S.p.A

3 5 7 9 8 6 4 2

For Mum
#BeMoreIsobel

To be a successful surgeon you need the eye of a hawk, the heart of a lion and the hands of a lady.

Doctor in the House, 1954

Prologue

As a trainee surgeon, it's all about the hernia. The inguinal hernia, to be precise. The operation starts when I shave a man's groin with a scalpel, and it always feels like a little bit of history. The original surgeons were barbers, and the red and white pole outside today's high-street barbers represents the bloody bandages used after the operation. I too am a barber surgeon.

After carefully removing any pubic hair, I become an artist. I paint his groin with a sponge soaked in Hibiscrub, a brown antiseptic solution, to sterilise his skin. I let it dry and then do it again before isolating the area with green cotton drapes.

But how did that man end up on my operating table? He came to see me with a lump in his groin. An inguinal hernia. They were the bane of my life as a medical student. The anatomy is complex and there are many terms that had to be memorised parrot-fashion for oral exams. A hernia happens when something inside the body, like fat or a loop of small bowel, pushes through a weakness in the muscle or surrounding tissue.

There's a natural weakness in the groin called the inguinal canal. It's a series of openings in the lower abdominal wall that the testicles travel down to reach the scrotum while a baby boy is still inside the womb. Trying to get my head around this three-dimensional canal from the flat pages of a book was hard. I just couldn't picture how everything fitted together. Instead, I practised by getting men to cough while I fumbled around in their groin trying to find a lump.

But there's an art to groin-fumbling. Although most hernias travel down the canal, called indirect hernias, sometimes the fat can push through a weakness in the back of the canal, causing a direct hernia. If I put my finger exactly halfway between their hip bone and the edge of their pubic bone and get a man to cough, I can tell which type of hernia they have. Either my finger controls the bulge, or the hernia pops out.

One of my bosses was a hernia expert. He would make me write down in the notes what kind of hernia I thought each man had. And then we would take him to theatre and see if I was right. To make things easier for the patient, I was taught to fix them using local anaesthetic. The patient was awake but didn't feel pain, only pressure. They could walk out of theatre and go home shortly afterwards instead of the longer recovery needed after a general anaesthetic. As great as it is for the patient, it is technically challenging for the surgeon. The first time I infiltrated the canal with anaesthetic, the tissues bulged with the fluid and the anatomy was distorted. And because the patient was awake, I had to watch what I said. No more asking the scrub nurse for a knife or a needle. We developed our own sign language instead.

In a few months I had done over fifty of them and was

left to crack on by myself. Back to the man on my table. After hanging a drape like a curtain in front of him to hide my handiwork, I pick up the blade and start to cut, gently dissecting through each individual layer, infiltrating with anaesthetic as I go.

Two of the other consultants wander into theatre to see what I'm up to. If it was any other operation, sweat would start to drip down the back of my legs at the pressure of being watched, but this is a hernia repair. They are teasing me, trying to put me off my game, but this is my field. They can't rile me. Not here. Not in my place.

I open up the inguinal canal and everyone peers into the wound.

'Yes!' I whisper to myself.

I was right. It's a direct hernia.

I smile under my mask as I carry on gently teasing out the hernia, pushing it back inside the abdomen where it belongs. The consultants leave to find other trainees to tease.

The nurse hands me a sterile mesh that I carefully cut to size, taking care to round the edges of the rectangle so there are no spiky corners, cutting a curve to match the patient's body, happy in my work. Like dressmaking, I tailor it to fit his groin. After a quick check on the patient to make sure he's OK, I suture in the mesh with a Prolene thread. It's bright blue and has a memory. It wants to curl up like it did in the suture packet, so I run it through my hand a few times to straighten it out. To coax it to behave. And then I tack the mesh to the underlying tissue with a simple running stitch, to keep it in place, before burying the knot.

I ask the man to cough to test my repair job. Not even a glimmer of a bulge. God, I'm good.

And then, my favourite bit. Closing up the wound. I carefully sew the layers of the canal back together. I start at either end, moving my way towards the middle so they are perfectly aligned.

I finish with the skin, pushing the needle just under the surface with a clear suture, taking little bites that can't be seen. The skin comes together with the smallest of humps in the middle that I know will heal as a beautiful, flat scar. My craftsmanship will soon be hidden by his pubic hair, but that's not the point. I remove the drapes. The scrub nurse hands me a large wet swab to clean the skin before applying a surgical dressing. It must be parallel to the wound. Nothing else is acceptable. I lower my mask, approach the end of the bed, and tell him it's all over.

He gives me a grin and says, 'Thank you, nurse.'

Chapter 1

There were twelve of us in the sixth form who wanted to study medicine. As part of our work experience, we were going to watch a friend's dad operate. A minibus picked us up and took us to the hospital. I couldn't believe how big it was. I'd only ever been to the tiny local one and this was huge – a mass of sprawling grey buildings. How did anyone ever find their way around inside? We were met at the entrance by a junior doctor who rushed us through a maze of stairs and corridors until we came to the operating department, where the theatre sister was waiting. 'Don't touch anything. Don't leave your valuables in the changing room. If you think you're going to faint, fall backwards. Remember: don't touch anything.'

There was a mad rush to grab some scrubs. I was swamped in an extra-large set and hoped that my trousers wouldn't end up around my ankles. I managed to find a pair of matching shoes but they were too small, smelled of sweaty feet and were covered in brown stains. After stuffing my hair into a theatre cap, it was time to go.

Leaving the changing room was like going through the wardrobe into Narnia. It was a whole new world. Everyone wore the same blue uniform. The only way to tell people apart was by the colour of their cap. The sister rounded us up. 'There are two rows of steps at the back. Stand on them. Keep quiet. And don't touch anything.' She crossed her hands over her ample bosom and nodded expectantly. We all followed suit and she nodded again. 'That's right,' she said. 'Remember: don't touch anything.' Then she let us inside.

The first thing that hit me was the smell of fresh blood, warm and sickly sweet. I gagged for a few seconds and then I could take in what was in front of me. The operating theatre was a large white room with a dark-blue floor. In the centre, underneath two big bright lights, was a narrow table. Lying on it was a man completely covered in emerald-green drapes with only a rectangle of abdominal skin visible. Two surgeons, their gowns spattered in blood, had their hands deep inside him. A nurse was passing them metal instruments and sutures from a draped trolley. At the head of the table, an anaesthetist was doing a crossword while his machine beeped in the background. My friend's dad eventually looked up and introduced himself. 'This man has bowel cancer and we're removing part of his colon. Here – look at this.' He lifted some of the small bowel out of the abdomen. It was pink and shiny. He flicked it with his finger, and I saw it move, wriggling as it dangled in the air. I was hooked.

The spell was broken by a loud thud as one of the boys hit the deck behind me, but it didn't distract me for long. Watching that operation was like being in the front row of a concert, seeing musicians play a symphony without needing a conductor to guide them. The pace picked up. I could feel the tension building until finally

6

the cancer was separated from the rest of the bowel and dropped into a large white bucket.

'Does anybody want to feel it?'

I thrust my hand straight up in the air. After a struggle with the tight latex gloves, I reached down into the bucket. The surface of the bowel was soft and smooth and still warm to touch while the cancer felt hard and gnarly, like a knot of wood. By the time I got back to my step the surgeons had finished and were closing the wound. It was time for us to go.

As I walked back to the changing room, I became aware of just how sore my feet were after standing in those tiny clogs for two hours, but I couldn't stop smiling. I'd found my calling. I was going to be a surgeon.

Chapter 2

I grew up surrounded by medicine. My dad was a surgeon before he became a GP and Mum had been one of the staff nurses on his ward. I was fascinated by his job. When he was on-call I would quietly creep into his study and eavesdrop when he talked to patients on the phone, trying to work out what was wrong with them. After a particularly bad weekend full of kids with viral illnesses, I thought I could have picked up the phone myself and told the parents what to do. Calpol, cool baths and flat lemonade. It seemed to solve everything.

When I was first taught about the human body in school, the teacher gave us the basics but I needed to know more. I would sit next to Dad on the sofa while he gave me extra lessons. I remember when he told me that the small bowel had three parts: the duodenum, jejunum and ileum. I loved saying the words out loud. It was a foreign language I was desperate to learn. I was curious about everything and remember asking Mum why I didn't fill up with water when I had a bath. I knew I had a hole down there and couldn't understand why it didn't let all the bathwater in. She was left trying to explain negative pressure to a frustrated seven-year-old.

9

Although my dad was a busy GP, he operated once a week helping a gynaecology consultant at the small local hospital. When I was eight or nine, I'd often tag along with him at the weekends when he went in to check on his post-op patients. I remember the first time I went. He parked outside the large red-brick building, and I held tightly on to his hand as he marched through the entrance, saying hello to everyone he passed. I struggled to keep up with him as he strode down the long corridor with its tiled blue floors and peeling white paint. I was fascinated by the strange sounds and smells, curious about the patients being pushed in wheelchairs ahead of us, desperate to know what was going on behind the closed doors.

Eventually, we reached his ward and I held on to his hand just a little tighter than before. I was going to see real patients. What would they look like? How would they smell? As we turned the corner, I could see two long rows of beds that faced each other. The men were closest to us, separated from the women by a curtain. I could smell the hot milk from the tea trolley. My trainers squeaked on the polished wooden floor as Dad took me to the nurses' station. They made a huge fuss of me and gave me a sherbet lemon to suck while he did his rounds. I knew that one day I would follow in his footsteps and have patients of my own.

I threw myself into my A-levels and got a place at Cardiff University to study medicine. I couldn't wait to start training to become a doctor, but I wasn't sure how I was going to cope living away from home. I'd never had to cook for myself or manage a budget. The only thing I knew how to do was study.

The first day of medical school began with an introduction from the Dean in a huge lecture theatre lined with wood. Once he'd finished, we were taken to the dissection room in the basement. There we were met by Owain, the larger-than-life man who ran the lab. He got up on to a chair and announced, 'No one enters this room without a lab coat. Take a manual and work out where your table is.'

We bustled into the changing room, swapping our jumpers and jackets for pristine white coats. I rummaged around in the bottom of my rucksack to find my dissecting kit – a brown canvas roll holding scalpel handles, tissue forceps, probes and scissors. There was a large white board with our names on, split alphabetically into groups of six. It was like a wedding reception but instead of flowers in the middle of each table there would be a body donated to medical science.

The first thing that hit me was the smell of formalin. It would permeate everything I owned for the next two years. It made my nose sting and my eyes water as I made my way to table one, tucked away at the back. Five others joined me, all strangers. There were twenty metal tables covered in large white plastic sheets hiding the bodies underneath. Owain swept around the room removing the sheets and suddenly I was face to face with a dead man. I was only eighteen. I'd never seen a naked man before, let alone a dead one. He was long and thin with white hair and waxy skin. There was a large bruise on his right thigh and I could see a faint appendix scar on his stomach. A brown cardboard tag had been tied to his left big toe with the number 'one' written on it.

'Welcome to medical school,' said Owain. 'Today you're starting with the arm. Follow the instructions for day one. Take it in turns. Always use a fresh blade. Every piece of tissue you remove goes in a black bin in the back with your table number on it.'

I spent three afternoons a week for the next two years slowly learning how the human body was put together. It was only by painstakingly following a nerve from the shoulder to the fingertips that I really understood how the arm worked. Every so often, Owain would gather us at one end of the room to show us something. One day, he lifted a pair of preserved conjoined twins from a bucket and the student next to him fainted. When we reached the pelvis, an amazing woman old enough to be my granny turned up as a guest demonstrator. She dissected a male pelvis so the students with female bodies could learn the male anatomy. I can still remember the wicked smile on her face as she took a scalpel to the cadaver's preserved erection.

Owain's pièce-de-résistance, though, was on the first day of our summer term. We filtered in as normal, waiting for the go-ahead to remove the plastic sheets. As we did, all I could hear was a loud thud, thud, thud – like a bad drum solo – as the tops of the skulls fell on the floor. The second-year students had removed the brains that morning. It would be our turn next year. And that year passed in a flash.

Before I could leave the dead behind and learn how to practise medicine on the living, there was the small matter of passing the basic science exams at the end of the second year. If I wasn't in a lecture theatre, I was in a library trying to memorise pages and pages of notes and understand the basic principles of physiology, anatomy and biochemistry. I struggled with anatomy at first. It's such a visual subject. To make things a bit easier, I had a skeleton to play with. Well, half a skeleton and a skull to be exact. He was called Fred. I bought him off a third-year student who no longer needed him. I spent hours sat on my bed running my fingers over the bones trying to remember where all the muscles and tendons attached. Every so often a tiny white spider would crawl out from one of the skull holes. That's when I went back to the library. I knew the exams would be hard and rarely went out, preferring to spend every spare moment I had in front of a textbook.

That all changed when the last exam was over. I hit the student union with my housemate Hannah and the rest of our year. I couldn't wait to get drunk and let my hair down. I had a moment of indecision at the bar as I tried to work out what to order. It had been such a long time since I'd had a drink. In the end, I went for two double vodkas and coke. I didn't like vodka, but I knew it would get me drunk. I meant to neck one and slowly drink the other, but I downed both and went back to the bar for more. After my fifth round, I started drinking from one of the lads' pints on the dancefloor. I don't remember anything after that. I came to in A&E attached to a drip with Hannah beside me and a strong smell of vomit in the air.

I woke up the next morning at home, fully clothed and blind as a bat. I couldn't find my glasses. They weren't on the bedside table where I normally put them. I sat up and groaned. My head was killing me, and a rush of bile came up into my mouth. I staggered into the kitchen to find Hannah sitting at the table. 'What happened?'

'You don't remember?'

'No. Do you know where my glasses are?'

'In your jacket pocket. Come and sit down, and I'll make you a cup of tea.'

As my hangover kicked in, I heard the sordid details. After bouncing around the dancefloor drinking other people's pints, I went missing. My friends split up to look for me and Hannah found me unconscious under one of the sofas at the back of the club. She had to call an ambulance because I was out cold. I'd vomited over her new velvet jacket in the back of the ambulance. The doctor in A&E gave me a bag of fluid to sober me up enough to go home.

I was dreading going into lectures on Monday as I knew the gossip would have spread. Bizarrely, however, it had earned me kudos among my peers. Two more of us had ended up in hospital over the weekend for the same thing but I was the first. I was almost proud. Alcohol poisoning had given me a new status. I wasn't a nerd anymore. I was a nerd who could drink.

The third year was divided up into five-week blocks rotating through all the different specialities and learning another language. Every patient admitted to the hospital had to be clerked. The house officer was the most junior doctor on the team, and I would tag along with them when they were on-call to learn how to do it. First, they took a history. This was a long list of questions asking the patient about the problem that had brought them into hospital, any other medical problems they had, the medications they were on, whether they drank or smoked, and how they coped at home. That was followed by a thorough examination of their heart, lungs, abdomen and nervous system before the jigsaw pieces were put together to come up with a diagnosis. Consultants would tell us that you should be able to work out what was wrong with someone just by talking to them.

Each team was known as a firm and at the end of every block there was always a firm do. On the last Thursday of the month, Cardiff restaurants were filled with medical students and every doctor in South Wales who wasn't on-call. When the meal was over, everyone went on to the Philharmonic nightclub. It wasn't unusual to see drunk consultants gyrating with students on the dancefloor. It was such a tradition that the local radio station promoted the club as the place to go if you wanted to pull a doctor. While Thursday nights were reserved for the Philly, Friday nights were always spent at MedClub, the medical-student union on the hospital campus. I started working behind the bar to earn a bit of money. I loved the power of being able to choose who I'd serve next, picking friends or boys I fancied over students I didn't know.

Back on the wards, it felt like I was always in the way. The junior doctors rarely had time to teach us. I got tired of being told to go and have coffee in the mess. Every hospital had one. It was a room where the doctors went to escape from the wards, grab a slice of toast and catch up on the gossip. I really did need to know how to examine patients, if only to survive the consultant ward round.

It was the main event of the week, and I never looked forward to it. First there was the chaotic shuffling as everyone squeezed in behind the blue curtain. We all thought that the student closest to the consultant would be picked on to examine the patient. No one wanted to go in first. I normally took the lead, hoping to get the humiliation over with quickly, but the consultants knew what we were up to. They would choose whoever was staring at the floor the hardest. No one was safe.

The fourth year was packed with lectures in pharmacology and pathology followed by another hideous exam. The stress of revising was getting to me. Everything seemed like a huge effort. Some days it was a struggle just to get out of bed in the morning. I felt like I was living in a thick black cloud. I wasn't sleeping well and my appetite disappeared. I'd start crying for no particular reason and would pretend I had a migraine so I could avoid going out with friends. After a few days the cloud would lift and I'd feel ready to face the world again. Hannah would lend me her lecture notes and life carried on as before.

The fifth year was spent back on the wards getting ready for Finals, the clinical exams we had to pass before we could qualify as doctors. Everyone was tested in medicine and surgery but the long cases could be in anything from gynaecology to paediatrics. During the psychiatry block I spent a lot of time clerking patients and started to wonder whether I had depression myself. I recognised the symptoms the patients were describing. I still had days where I felt very low but I couldn't hide in my room anymore because the consultants monitored our attendance on the wards. I forced myself to plaster a smile on my face and pretend that everything was fine. I told myself it wasn't really depression, just the stress of finals. Everything would be OK once the exams were over.

When I wasn't observing in clinic, I'd ask house officers for interesting cases. I'd rush off to the patient who sounded the best, hoping I'd get there first and they'd let me practise examining them. They must have seen five or ten students every day and most of them put up with us. Some even told us how to do it properly.

'The doctor normally puts his stethoscope here, love.'

'Shall I cough for you?'

'You've got to push a bit harder. It doesn't hurt.'

They were the experts after all, and I filled a notebook with lumps and murmurs and wheezes.

Back at home, Hannah and I would practise on each other, memorising the phrases we needed to describe what we'd found. As finals got closer, one of the registrars gave us tips on how to pass the clinical exams. Registrars are in the last stage of their training. She had chosen to specialise in respiratory medicine and was in the middle of a six-year rotation to learn everything she needed to know to work as a consultant. 'It's all a game,' she said. 'You have to over-exaggerate everything so the examiner can see that you know what you're doing. If you're nervous, hesitate or question what you're saying, you won't pass. Besides, you're going to be doing it for real in a month's time. They're looking for someone who will write down a diagnosis and plan in the notes, instead of a list of tentative suggestions.'

I'd forgotten that I was going to be a doctor at the end of all of this.

'One more thing,' she said. 'You need to be able to describe what you've found without using your hands. Liz, if you describe a breast lump and your hands go up to your chest, the consultant is now staring at your cleavage instead of listening to what you're saying. It's also good practice for when you're calling someone for an opinion. They can't see your hands through the phone.'

If the stress of passing finals wasn't enough, I also had to apply for two Pre-Registration House Officer posts. Every junior doctor had to do six months of general medicine and general surgery as a PRHO before they were fully registered with the General Medical Council. Most of us wanted to stay in Wales. I was desperate to get the only surgical job attached to a professorial unit on a breast and thyroid cancer firm. I knew the reference would look good on my CV in the future, but that wasn't the only reason I wanted the job. Half of the job involved covering paediatric surgery. I'd spent time on the firm in my final year and had fallen in love with the speciality. It was true general surgery, covering everything from a tiny premature baby born with its bowel lying outside its abdomen to a teenager with a kidney tumour. As an added bonus, the consultant had a reputation for letting his house officers operate. When I'd previously shadowed house officers in general surgery, they were always so busy on the wards that they never saw the inside of an operating theatre.

I worked hard for the interviews and got the medical job I wanted as well. All I had to do was pass finals. Five years of knowledge was condensed into a handful of exams that would determine whether I'd be starting work as a doctor in a month's time. When the last exam was over, we all went to MedClub to wait for the results to be posted on the noticeboard. You could cut the tension with a knife. Finally, one of the administrators appeared and started pinning up the sheets of paper, and all hell broke loose. If your name wasn't on the list, you'd failed. It was chaos as everyone tried to get to the front. Hannah shouted back to me that I'd passed but I had to see it for myself. Eventually, I saw my name, right there in black and white. I could now call myself Dr Ball.

Chapter 3

The day had finally arrived when I would have patients of my own to look after. My first job was in paediatric surgery and now that I was actually going to have to look after tiny babies, I was terrified. Most of my time on the wards as a student had been spent looking after the elderly and the reality of paediatrics was daunting. Luckily, I had two senior house officers to help me as well as the registrar, Tom. I wanted to be the female version of him. He was great with the kids, confident with the parents and loved by the nurses.

I was rostered to be on-call for the first weekend. It would be my second day as a doctor. The shift started on Friday morning, and I wouldn't go home until the following Monday. I hoped it would be quiet. After the morning ward round to see the children going to theatre, my boss told me that the first case on the list was mine. It was an eleven-year-old boy who needed an appendicectomy.

'Seriously?' I asked.

'Yes. Seriously.'

I couldn't believe it. I was actually going to do an operation. My mind was racing. On the one hand I was desperately trying to recall the steps of the operation and on the other I was panicking over what to do if my bleep went off when I was scrubbed.

The consultant took me into the operating room and introduced me to the theatre team. He then took the batteries out of my bleep and told the nurse in charge to deal with it. After he'd scrubbed up with Tom, it was my turn. The five minutes it took to scrub my nails and wash my hands felt like forever. My glasses were steaming up because I hadn't pinched the nose of my mask tight enough and I was all fingers and thumbs trying to get gloves on while keeping my hands inside the sleeve cuff of the gown.

I pushed the scrub room door open with the back of my shoulder, holding my hands in front of my face to keep them sterile. I felt sick with nerves. Someone reached inside my gown from the back to tie it closed. I grabbed the waist ties at the front, holding on to one while I passed the assistant the other. I twirled to wrap the gown around my waist. Once I'd tied the ends in a knot, I approached the table. The lights were turned on. The stage was set.

A small square of skin stained pink by the disinfectant was waiting for me, surrounded by green drapes. All I could hear were the background beeps of the anaesthetic machine. The scrub nurse passed me a blade. I looked at my consultant. He nodded. I knew what to do. I'd seen it done before. I turned to look at the anaesthetist and asked him, 'Are you happy?'

'Yes.'

There was no turning back. My boss stood next to me, elbow to elbow, hip to hip. Tom and the scrub nurse were opposite. Feeling the reassuring weight of the scalpel in my hand, I took a steadying breath. I knew where to cut.

I'd read the books. But I was paralysed. Could I actually cut into a child? I pressed against the skin. It was like a hot knife going through butter. I switched to diathermy – an electric pen that uses a high frequency current to cut tissue and cauterise bleeding vessels. I worked my way through the layers of fascia and muscle until I could see the thin layer of peritoneum glistening beneath. After making a small hole in it, all I had to do was find the appendix inside. I wriggled my finger around trying to find something that felt like a worm. I stretched up on my tiptoes twisting my arm around, sweeping my finger back and forth along his abdominal wall when I suddenly felt it. 'Wow. It does feel like a worm!'

'Good. Now break down the adhesions and bring it out of the wound.'

After Tom had divided the blood vessels and tied two sutures around the base of the appendix, the consultant passed me the scalpel so I could finish the job. I triumphantly dropped it in the receiving dish, grinning from ear to ear. I'd done an operation. In my first week as a junior doctor. Life would never be the same again.

I dragged my housemates to the pub to celebrate, and as I headed to the bar, I bumped into one of the surgical registrars who'd taught me at med school.

'How's it going?'

'I've just done my first appendix! God, I love surgery.'

'Good for you. But are you a real surgeon?' He leaned forward and whispered in my ear, 'Did you get an erection?'

I watched him swagger back to his friends, no doubt thinking he'd shocked me. But I got it. The thrill. The power. The release. I knew this was all I wanted to do for the rest of my life.

The remainder of the weekend had been uneventful. I'd admitted a couple of children with appendicitis and that was it. On Sunday night, a GP rang me about a twelve-year-old boy with an acute abdomen. At ten o'clock, the ward bleeped me to let me know he'd arrived. When I got to his room he was crying in pain, and I could tell the nurses were worried. His abdomen was swollen on one side. I asked the nurse, 'How much does he weigh?'

'Forty kilograms.'

'Can you draw up five milligrams of morphine and hang a bag of fluid?'

His mum told me that he'd had complex abdominal surgery for cancer when he was little. I'd never heard of the reconstructive operation she described and couldn't get my head around what had been done. All I knew was that he was sick and I didn't know why. The nurse came back with the drugs and fluids.

'The lab phoned. His white count, CRP and lactate are up.'

That wasn't good. He was septic. Right. Think. Bowel obstruction? Bowel perforation? I looked at my watch. It was now 11 p.m. I bleeped the general surgical registrar covering paediatrics for the night but he didn't answer; I tried calling theatres and they said he was scrubbed and would be busy for hours. The porter finally arrived to take the boy for an X-ray and all I could do was wait.

When he came back to the ward, I held the film up to the light box in his room. There was no free air so at least the young boy hadn't perforated. The nurse came in to check his obs. 'He's still in a lot of pain.'

'Give him some more morphine and fluids. I'll be back in an hour.'

I needed a change of scene to try and work out what to do next. After inhaling a slice of toast in the mess I went back to the ward. It was now 1 a.m. I spent the rest of the night pacing back and forth, checking on him every hour. I flicked though the textbooks in the office looking for help, for hope. He'd needed several doses of morphine overnight, and by the time dawn was breaking, he'd started to vomit.

At 8 a.m. sharp, the team strode on to the ward. I rushed out of his room to explain what had happened. My consultant took one look at him and held up his X-ray.

'Get a lateral decubitus film now.'

One of the senior house officers rang radiology. I whispered to Tom, 'What's that?'

'If a kid is too sore to stand up for the X-ray then you can miss free air. A decubitus film is done on their side. It can often pick up a hidden perforation.'

The new X-ray came back and there was a clear line of air at the top of the film. Shit. He'd had a bowel perforation all along and I'd missed it. What would happen to him now? What would happen to me?

My boss took him straight to theatre, interrupting the general surgeons who were about to send for their first emergency case of the day. I asked if I could stay to watch, even though I should have gone home hours ago. I had to see this through.

Tom opened him up and my heart sank. All I could see was a large coil of purple small bowel, like a massive black pudding. It was dead. All of it. I could see the anger on my consultant's face.

'Come here and look inside.'

I peered into the boy's abdomen. Tom moved the coils of dead bowel out of the way to show a tiny adhesion deep inside. A thin film of tissue only a few millimetres wide had formed around the small bowel creating a closed loop of dead gut. After clamping the black bowel, my boss snipped the adhesion. It took less than a second.

'Why didn't you call me?'

'The night reg was busy and I didn't want to wake you.'

My boss looked down at me, peered over his mask and said, 'I'm the one paid to worry, not you. Any time. Day or night. You call me. I know you did what you thought was right, but this boy will now have to be fed by a tube for the rest of his life.'

The consequences of my actions dawned on me. That boy would never eat normally again because he'd had most of his small bowel removed. Burgers and chips would now be replaced by a white viscous fluid pumped into his stomach through a tube. He'd been through so much already in his short life and it was my fault it was about to get a whole lot worse. I stepped away from the table and sank to the floor. What had I done?

It took forever to walk home. I dropped my bag on the floor, sat down and started crying. I couldn't stop. No one else was home. I pulled myself up the stairs and crawled under the duvet, still fully dressed, hoping that sleep would come and save me from the memory of the night before. Seventy-two hours after my first appendicectomy and I wanted to pack it all in.

I wasn't the only one struggling. Lorna, one of my close friends, was working with a surgeon in a different hospital who summoned her to help in theatre on her second week in the job. Once she was scrubbed, her boss said to his registrar, 'We're going to need to teach Lorna the Penny Procedure.'

'What's that?' she said.

'I don't want to dig you in the ribs while I'm operating. My last house officer, Penny, was very well endowed and it seemed logical to rest my elbow on her cleavage. Hence, the Penny Procedure.' He didn't give Lorna the chance to say no. She was so upset that no one in the room had said anything when it happened. It was as if this behaviour was normal and we were simply meant to put up with it in exchange for a good reference at the end of the job.

When I wasn't on-call, I was out drinking and dancing with friends. It was so nice having money to spend instead of living on a student budget. I no longer had to buy the cheapest wine. However, the highs of the job brought terrible lows. The black days had never gone away and were getting closer and closer together. I did my best to hide them but one afternoon I found myself crying in the sluice room for no reason at all. It finally dawned on me that this wasn't normal. I needed help. My GP started me on antidepressants, and I hoped things would improve. They would take a couple of weeks to work, but just knowing that I'd soon feel normal again made it easier to cope. I now looked forward to the challenge of putting in tiny cannulas in even tinier babies and got better at looking after the neonatal patients. It was mind-blowing to watch Tom and my boss operate on babies who'd been born with their organs outside their abdomen or a huge hole in their diaphragm. The children were often premature and it amazed me how these men with their massive hands could perform such delicate surgery. It was like watching grand masters at work as they gently manipulated such fragile tissue with the smallest of instruments. I had fallen in love with the speciality all over again and was already working out what senior house officer (SHO) jobs I'd have to do if I wanted to join them. However, it was time to move on to general surgery.

Chapter 4

I turned up on the ward for my first day in general surgery and realised I'd already made a mistake. All the
other doctors were wearing white coats and I'd left mine
at home. No one had worn them in paediatrics. I picked
up my new bleep and the handover sheet from the ward
receptionist when I heard my name.

'It's Liz, isn't it? Nice to meet you. Let's go.'

It was John, my new SHO. He was in a rush to get the
ward round done before heading off to theatre. I was left
with a list of jobs and clear instructions for the patients
coming in later. I was still clerking when he found me on
the ward at six o'clock. He'd come to consent the patients
for tomorrow's list. Everyone having an operation had to
sign a form to say that they had been told what operation
they were having, why they were having it and any
potential side effects and complications of the surgery.
'Are you on-call tomorrow?'

'Yes,' I said.

'Me too. Get some rest.'

Just like in paediatrics, I was on-call for my first weekend. That night I carefully packed the pockets of my
white coat with everything I thought I'd need – pens,

tourniquets, blood forms, gloves and a bar of chocolate in case I didn't have time to eat. The final thing I squeezed in was the *Oxford Handbook of Clinical Medicine*. It told me how to treat anything. There was even a page explaining what to do if I dropped my bleep in the toilet.

I joined John and the registrar for the ward round but halfway through my bleep went off. I rushed to find a phone, my heart racing. It was a local GP referring a sixty-year-old man with a fresh rectal bleed. I rang the admissions unit to let them know and then started to panic. I couldn't remember how to treat it. I flicked through the handbook as I went back to find John but the ward round had moved on. I bleeped him, pacing in front of the phone until he eventually answered. 'What do I do?'

'Have you seen the patient?'

'No.'

'Well, go and see him and call me when you're done.'

I was imagining the worst as I made my way to the admissions unit. I started walking faster, clinging on to my pockets to stop things falling out. I burst through the doors, expecting a flurry of activity around my dying patient. Instead, I saw a nurse at the desk chatting to a porter over a cup of tea. 'I'm the surgical house officer. There's a patient for me?'

'That's right. He's in room three. Here's the letter.'

As I scanned the referral I let out a huge sigh of relief. The patient I'd feared was bleeding to death simply had piles. He was delighted to see me and launched into a long and complicated story that I dutifully wrote down. When he finally finished, I went to find a nurse to act as a chaperone. It was time to do my first rectal exam. 'Can you pull your pants down and roll on to your left-hand side?' I asked. 'Now curl your knees up to your chest.'

I scrabbled around in the trolley to find some K-Y jelly and squeezed a large dollop on to my finger. As I bent down for a closer look I could see three large purple grapes bulging from his backside. I tried to push my finger past them but he yelped in pain. I felt awful for making things worse. Apologising, I wiped away the jelly.

All I had left to do was put in a venflon. It's a plastic cannula that stays in a vein that nurses use to give intravenous drugs and fluids. I thought this would be easy after my time in paediatrics. I reached for the small pink one I always used in children. He had a lovely vein on the back of his hand, but instead of going inside, the cannula skidded around it. A bloody bruise had already started to form.

'Ow. That hurts.'

'Sorry.' I found another vein and tried again but the same thing happened. I could tell by the look on his face that he was getting frustrated.

'I'll get someone else to come and have a go.'

I bleeped John, feeling like a failure. I could hear the sounds of the staff dining room in the background. I'd obviously interrupted his coffee break and felt more guilty. John got the cannula in first time. He said, 'You need to use a bigger cannula. The needle is sharper and it's easier to get in. Can you prescribe some lidocaine jelly for the piles and ask a nurse to put some ice cubes in a rubber glove for him to sit on? It helps to get the swelling down. I'll catch up with you in a couple of hours or so. Remember to have some lunch.'

John and I didn't stop that weekend. There was a constant stream of cases coming through the doors. Appendicitis, cholecystitis, diverticulitis, abscesses that needed draining and ulcers that needed debriding. John was kept busy in theatre while I learned my place was either in the admissions unit clerking or in the mess wolfing down hot buttered toast before I got bleeped again. I was enjoying trying to work out what was wrong with the patients I saw and loved it when the bloods and X-rays confirmed I was right. By Sunday night my coat was no longer crisp and white. The once organised pockets were now stuffed full of blood forms. A messy row of sticky labels ran up my arm from the patients I'd seen earlier. It was midnight and I was ready to collapse when my bleep went off. It was John. 'There's an aneurysm in resus.'

Resus was the resuscitation area of A&E where the critically ill patients were taken. When the aorta is diseased it can stretch like a balloon and form an aneurysm. The bigger the aneurysm, the more likely it is to burst. And if someone with an aneurysm was in resus, it had almost certainly ruptured. The only thing that can save the patient is an immediate operation. Even then, many don't make it. I'd seen one as a student and it hadn't ended well. I rushed down to A&E to find John scribbling in the notes. He said, 'Call theatres and tell them the anaesthetist will meet us up there. Then run these bloods to the lab while I go and talk to his wife.'

I glanced at the patient. The pulsating mass in his abdomen was visible from the end of the bed. I tucked a blanket around him to keep him warm. I leaned in close and held his hand. 'Don't worry,' I said. We're going to look after you.' John came back. 'Liz, haven't you gone yet? The lab is waiting for the bloods.' My bleep went off. Another GP referral waiting to be seen. The registrar arrived to help John push the patient to theatre while I ran off in the other direction to the labs, gutted that I wouldn't be able to stay and watch the surgery.

I finally made it up to my on-call room at 3 a.m. and started to shiver. The window wouldn't close and the room was icy cold. I collapsed on to the narrow bed, the sheets still sweaty from the night before, and pulled the blanket tight around my ears in an effort to keep out the draught. Half an hour later, my bleep went off. It was the registrar.

'We need you in theatre now. The aneurysm graft blew on the way to Intensive Care but John's in resus with another emergency.'

I stumbled out of bed, ran downstairs to theatre and got scrubbed.

The consultant passed me a large metal retractor holding the liver and small bowel out of the way. 'Hold this. Don't move.'

I could see that the aorta was crumbling as he tried to sew another graft on. It looked more like cheese than a blood vessel. As I peered over to get a closer look, the retractor slipped.

'For fuck's sake. Don't move.'

My curiosity meant he'd lost his view at a critical moment. I braced myself, holding on to the retractor for dear life. The next thing I remember is someone trying to take it off me.

'You can let go now. We need to close.'

I'd fainted at the table. The exhaustion of the weekend

combined with the sudden dash to theatre had been too much. The only thing stopping me hitting the deck was the retractor I was clinging on to. I stepped back and slid to the floor, ripping off my mask. It was now 7.30. Time to get ready for the morning handover.

I now had my own medical students to teach on the wards and it took a while to get used to the shift in power. One year ago, I was in awe of the confident house officers I shadowed. Now that I was one myself, I didn't think I was all that powerful. I had never realised just how busy the job would be, and sparing even half an hour to go through a case could add another hour on to the end of my day as I worked my way through the tasks that had piled up while I was teaching. I did my best to teach them and tell them how to survive in theatre. One consultant in the hospital was notorious for shouting at students and I'd seen friends suffer when he lost his temper.

'If you want to be allowed to watch a case,' I said, 'you have to know the patient. How old they are, what their job is, what their symptoms are.' The students nodded earnestly as they scribbled in their notebooks. 'You also need to know how to treat the problem they have and what the operation involves. If you turn up without doing your homework, he'll kick you out of theatre.'

I'd heard as a student that the only way to learn medicine was to hang a disease on a patient. Now I was telling my own students the same. 'Trust me, it's the only way to learn. You may forget how to treat pancreatitis after reading a textbook, but you'll never forget Mrs Davies who got gallstones when she was pregnant and then spent a week on ITU with pancreatic necrosis.'

One of the consultants I worked for when I was on-call had a particular way with words and a lot of my time was spent with John on a second ward round as we explained to the patients what was actually going to happen. The consultants were always in a rush to get to clinic or theatre, and it was up to us to fill in the details. One weekend an elderly gentleman had been admitted with a bowel obstruction due to a cancer he didn't know he had. The consultant examined him, looked at his scans and then said, 'There's badness in the belly, old chap. It's cancer, but don't worry, I'll fix it for you.' And off he went. John had to explain that fixing it meant an operation and a permanent colostomy.

Thanks to the antidepressants my mood was improving and I was learning to love general surgery. I got quicker at clerking and very good at eating takeaways in five minutes, standing to put my plate in the sink as I swallowed the final mouthful. But most of all, I got better at getting the diagnosis right. There was nothing quite like presenting the case to the consultant the next day and hearing them say, 'Next patient.' It didn't happen very often but when it did, it made my heart sing.

Senior house officer jobs were about to be advertised and I needed to decide what rotation to apply for when my medical house jobs finished. I knew that if I wanted to pursue a career in paediatric surgery I'd have to take a couple of years out to do pure paediatric and neonatal medicine. As much as I'd enjoyed working with children, I couldn't bear the thought of spending two years not operating. I wanted to be in theatre. It had to be general surgery.

The first year of every SHO rotation was normally split between A&E and general surgery while the second and third could be in anything from orthopaedics to neurosurgery. I wanted to stay in South Wales. I knew the hospitals and I knew which consultants I wanted to work for.

The interview fell on a Monday after yet another hideous weekend on-call. I got home, showered, changed into my suit and sat on the sofa flicking through my notes. I woke up with a jolt sometime later and looked at my watch.

'Shit.'

It was five minutes after my interview slot. Panicking, I rang Human Resources.

'I was meant to have an SHO interview this morning, but I overslept. I was on-call over the weekend and didn't stop. I'm really, really, sorry. Is there any way they could fit me in?'

'Let me find out. I'll call you back.'

Ten minutes later, the phone rang.

'You're in luck. They'll squeeze you in. Can you get here in twenty minutes?'

It was a good fifteen-minute walk to the hospital. I grabbed my keys and ran out the door trying to speed walk in heels. I made it in the nick of time, sweaty and breathless and nowhere near the cool, calm, collected woman I'd been hoping to portray. Despite everything, I was offered a job. It meant I could stay in Cardiff with Daljit and Bethan, two of my closest friends. But best of all, I could finally learn to operate. I just needed to get my medical house job out of the way.

Chapter 5

My first day in general medicine couldn't have got off to a worse start. I'd just met my new team and the ward round had started when my bleep went off. The consultant glared at me as I made my excuses and went to find a phone. It was Occupational Health telling me they couldn't clear me until I'd been assessed by one of their consultants.

It turned out that because I'd put on my health questionnaire that I was taking antidepressants, they needed to make sure I was safe to work. The doctor asked me a long list of probing questions about my depression. He then asked whether I was getting enough sleep. That made me laugh. I was working hundred-hour weeks with every third weekend on-call. Sleep was a luxury I rarely had. He had no idea what my life was like. I was so embarrassed and hated being scrutinised. I swore to myself that I would never mention depression on a health form again.

I wasn't expecting to enjoy working in general medicine. It was simply something I had to get through before I could get back to theatre. My first three months were going to be spent in respiratory medicine. Instead of doing rectal exams and checking post-op drains, I now spent my days taking arterial blood samples from patients with bronchitis and emphysema to check their carbon dioxide levels before tweaking the levels of oxygen they were on. Pneumonia took the lives of many of my patients, and although I now faced death on a regular basis, I never got used to it. I was in the bereavement office so often that Susan, the lady who ran it, became a firm friend.

Late one afternoon, I'd just buttered some toast in the mess when I got fast-bleeped to the nurses' office.

'What's up?'

'The lady in side-room three has died.'

'And?'

'Her family are with her and she was still for resus.'

'Shit. I'm on my way.'

The lady had come in with metastatic lung cancer and the plan was to get her symptoms under control so she could go home to die. No one had discussed CPR with her so if her heart stopped beating, the cardiac arrest team were meant to be called to try and bring her back. I went to find the nurse looking after her. 'She looked like she was fast asleep when I went in but I couldn't feel a pulse. She was awake half an hour ago when the family arrived. I told them that she might have taken a turn for the worse and that I'd get a doctor to come and check on her.'

'What on earth do I do now?'

'No idea.'

I knocked on the door and introduced myself to the family. 'Would you mind leaving so I can quickly examine her?'

She was definitely dead. I waited for a minute to check that there were no signs of life and then let the family back in. Thinking on my feet, I said, 'She's slipped into a coma and is fading fast. It might be kinder to let her go in her sleep, given everything she's been through. What do you think?' They'd been expecting the news after the nurse's warning shot and agreed that letting her die peacefully was the right thing to do. 'I'll leave you alone now,' I said and went back to the nurses' office. 'If you go back in about ten minutes, you can then say that she's died. Let's hope we get away with it.' Luckily, we did.

I shared each on-call shift with another house officer. One of us covered the acute intake of medical emergencies while the other dealt with the wards and any patients who'd taken an overdose. Many didn't know what they'd taken, and I'd spend hours with the team trying to decipher what the little white tablets could be. There were many heartbreaking cases, and it was awful when I had to tell a family that their loved one hadn't survived, especially when they were young.

One night I went to clerk a woman in her fifties who'd drunk two bottles of vodka with diazepam, and she took an instant dislike to me. I backed away from her as she started shouting and swearing, hoping that the security guard outside would come to my rescue. The next thing I knew she lashed out, punching me on the chin, sending me and the guard behind the curtain flying. I never went in to see a patient without a chaperone after that.

When I was on call, I realised that surgery had been a breeze compared to medicine. Instead of twelve to fifteen patients, I could see up to forty people during a shift. The record was seventy-two admissions, on Boxing Day. I was rarely on with the same SHO because of the way the rota worked, but I had my favourites. Megan was the best. She was confident and caring and would always check to see how I was. I normally saw the straightforward cases – mini-strokes, chest infections and indigestion. While I was peeling crusty socks off old men whose toe-nails had curled over, Megan would see the exciting stuff in the room next door – heart attacks and bleeding ulcers. One April weekend we were swamped. The registrar was looking after a university student with meningitis and Megan was busy dealing with a woman with a dangerously fast heart rate. I was about to eat my share of the cold takeaway delivered hours ago when a taxi driver pulled up outside. One of the nurses muttered, 'What's he doing? We're not A&E. He can't drop off a patient here.'

He staggered out of the car, pushed the doors open and collapsed. We managed to haul him on to a trolley and rushed him into a room.

'Can't. Breathe.'

An inhaler fell out of his trouser pocket and dropped on to the floor. I listened to his chest. I couldn't hear anything. A warning bell rang in the back of my mind. A silent chest in an asthmatic is a medical emergency. The nurses connected him up to a monitor and we could barely get an oxygen trace. Shit.

'Nebulisers. Now.' I raced next door. 'Megan, I've got an asthmatic who can't breathe.'

'OK. You take over here.'

We swapped patients and I got up to speed. Megan had given her drugs to slow her heart rate down and she was waiting for a chest X-ray. I was writing up more fluids when a high-pierced alarm sounded. I turned around to see the nurse feeling the woman's neck.

'No pulse.'

'Call the crash team.' I started doing chest compressions as the nurse from Megan's room came running in to help. She grabbed the oxygen mask. 'Megan can't leave. He's too sick.'

I prayed that the rest of the team would arrive soon. I'd never run a cardiac arrest by myself and had never had to shock anyone alone. 'Time?'

'One minute.'

'Pulse?'

'It's VF.' That meant ventricular fibrillation: the heart muscles twitch instead of squeeze, so blood isn't pumped around the body and it can kill without treatment.

'We need to shock her.' I grabbed the paddles and training took over. I'd just given the second shock when the rest of the crash team arrived. I was relieved to hand over to someone who knew what they were doing. After three rounds of CPR, the patient came back and was taken to ITU. Megan popped her head around the door and asked, 'Everything OK?'

'It is now. How's your man?'

'Stable at the moment but it was touch and go.'

'Tea?'

'Yes please.' And then my bleep went off again.

After three months I switched to general medicine and instead of dealing with chest infections and asthma, I was now looking after patients with angina, liver disease and strokes. The ward rounds took even longer than before and I spent what felt like hours listening to my registrar and consultant discuss whether to increase someone's beta-blocker based on the latest trial data. Afternoons were spent filling out forms and chasing results. I felt more like a secretary than a doctor.

There were more consultants than junior doctors in the hospital, so I ended up working for two at a time. One had a special interest in liver disease and hated having to treat anything else. Each time he saw a new patient who didn't have jaundice or hepatomegaly (an enlarged liver), he would run through a list of every medical consultant in the hospital. If the patient recognised one of the names, he would insist on referring them to that consultant, even if it had been twenty years since they'd last been seen in clinic. One day I presented a fifty-three-year-old man with textbook symptoms of a heart attack. His ECG confirmed it.

'What do you think, Liz? Has he had a heart attack?'

'I think so.'

'And what do we do with heart attacks?'

'Refer to another team?'

'Excellent. Next.'

He then moved on to the next patient. The registrar had to whisper to the nurse to ignore what he said because we would be looking after the patient after all.

The other consultant had his own distinctive way of explaining things to patients. One morning I was sat in clinic with him while he reviewed another man in his fifties with acute angina. The patient asked why it had happened.

'There are three reasons,' replied my boss. 'You drink, you smoke and you're pregnant.'

The patient looked confused until the penny dropped. He was morbidly obese and that was how my boss shocked patients into realising they needed to lose weight.

One weekend I was on-call with a geriatrician. We had to see an elderly man with Parkinson's disease and pneumonia. He also had ankylosing spondylitis, which meant that his neck was fused and he could only look down at the floor. He was seriously ill and there was a strong chance that he wouldn't survive this admission. I watched as the consultant sat on the floor so he could look up at this man and make eye contact while he spoke to him. He held his hand and offered to call his wife and let her know what was going on. It was such a change from my own two bosses. I knew which man I was going to copy when I started breaking bad news myself.

As the end of my medical job drew closer, my thoughts turned to the surgical exams I had to pass to become a Member of the Royal Colleges of Surgeons of Great Britain and Ireland – the MRCS. I had to pass both parts during my SHO rotation so I could get a registrar job at the end. I paid the £1,000 entrance fee and spent all my free time poring over past papers and textbooks. Although I was glad I'd spent time on the medical wards and knew it would help me to manage post-op patients with angina and pneumonia in the future, I couldn't wait to move back to the surgical world.

Chapter 6

The first job in my SHO rotation was in A&E medicine. I was one of thirteen junior doctors working in a brand-new unit. The first two days were spent getting a crash course in advanced life support, how to read X-rays, deal with fractures and close wounds. At the end I was given a thick instruction manual and then it was time to face the music.

Each twenty-four-hour period was split into three shifts and between us we covered four areas – minor injuries, paediatrics, major injuries and resus. My first shift was in majors, where anyone needing to lie on a trolley was sent. I walked on to the unit ready to go, only to find it was empty.

'Where are all the patients?'

'They've all gone to the wards or gone home,' said the nurse. 'Enjoy it while it lasts.'

Unlike the wards where there was always a list of outstanding jobs, for the first time in my working life I literally had nothing to do. Five minutes later, three patients were wheeled in and I didn't stop for the rest of the shift.

Working in A&E was terrifying and exhilarating and

tedious all at once. I quickly learned that the only way to survive was to ask the nurses everything. There was nothing they didn't know. I loved being part of a team pulling together to get the patients in and out of the department as quickly as possible. Covering majors also meant covering resus. There were two of us on each shift and we took it in turns to go when the bat phone went off. It was a bright-red phone that the paramedics used to warn us they were on their way with a critically ill patient. I saw everything come through those doors but it was the trauma I loved the most. I got high on the thrill of it. And as much as I loved the initial management, stabilising the patient and working out what they'd broken, putting chest drains in lungs full of blood and diagnosing ruptured spleens, I was incredibly jealous of the surgical SHOs, who got to take them to theatre. I would stare longingly as they left the department, hoping I'd see them before I went home to find out what had happened.

The paramedics were a vital part of the team and an important source of food on night shifts. Most of them were happily married but it didn't stop us flirting in exchange for chocolate from the late-night garage. One of the registrars told us to always trust the paramedics if they had a hunch about a patient. One afternoon, I was seeing someone in resus. He'd been watching a rugby match when he suddenly developed severe upper back pain and shortness of breath. As I looked at the notes the paramedic had taken, he said, 'I reckon he's had an aortic dissection.'

'Really?' I said. I'd never seen one and had only read

about them in textbooks. A tear occurs in the inner layer of the aorta causing blood to surge through it and split the layers of the aorta apart. It can be fatal.

'His pulse felt weaker on the left.'

I checked both wrists. It was weaker on the left. I asked the nurse to check the blood pressure in both arms and went to look at his chest X-ray. His aorta was a lot wider than it should be. The paramedic was just about to leave but I called him back.

'Come and look. I think you're right. Have you seen one before?'

'No. This is my first.'

Most of the patients who'd had a cardiac arrest in the community didn't survive. Although we would often do CPR for over an hour, they were just too sick. It was so hard to tell their loved ones, but unlike most relatives on the wards, the families were now grateful for everything we had done. I felt uncomfortable when they thanked me because I still worried that I hadn't done enough. There was only one occasion when I got shouted at. A ninety-year-old man with metastatic lung cancer had arrested at home. His wife had popped out to the shops but his niece was staying with him and she rang for an ambulance. He lived just around the corner from the hospital and an ambulance was there in minutes. I was on bat-phone duty and got the team ready to pounce the minute he arrived. A nurse started CPR and I ordered the first round of drugs. We got a pulse; I couldn't believe it. This was the first man I had ever brought back to life. I was on cloud nine. His wife arrived and she was furious.

Apparently, he hadn't wanted to be resuscitated and

had wanted to die at home but his niece didn't know. He spent the next three days being ventilated in ITU before his life support was switched off.

I was now starting to feel like a proper doctor. Patients would arrive who were seriously ill and I was able to make them better. It was amazing to be able to give someone with severe heart failure a concoction of drugs and watch them go from gasping for breath to being able to talk to me. It was such a rush. I became confident in running trauma calls whenever there had been a serious traffic accident, directing the other doctors and nurses to examine the patient and arrange the necessary tests.

In minor injuries, the days involved seeing patients with coughs and colds that didn't need antibiotics, while the nights were full of drunken girls who had sprained their ankles tottering around in heels trying to get a taxi home. On Sunday mornings, if I was the only woman on duty, it was my job to go fishing. Armed with a speculum and a long pair of sponge forceps I would pull out lost condoms and forgotten tampons. For a few months I saw a stream of underage girls with the cap from a deodorant bottle stuck inside them. Word had spread around a school that it would be safer to use a can of Impulse instead of having actual sex. I had to refer most of them on to the gynaecologists as I didn't have the necessary tools to pull the lids out.

One thing I did love about minor injuries was the stitching. It was the closest I got to operating and it meant a bit of peace and quiet as I sat in the suture room closing whatever came my way. One moment I would be gluing a rugby head-wound together and the next I'd be using the finest cobweb-like thread to repair the nail bed of a child who'd caught their finger in a car door.

At the weekends, the waiting rooms were full of drunken football and rugby supporters and it took ingenuity to keep rival fans apart. It was easy enough to patch them up but it was much harder to get rid of them. Many had travelled from far and wide for the game and by the time I'd seen them, their transport home was long gone. They expected us to pay for a taxi to take them home and could get quite violent when I explained that, although the NHS was good, it wasn't that good.

In the winter, my shifts were spent dealing with broken ankles, wrists and hips. One Sunday, the department was bursting at the seams. It seemed like the whole world had gone to church and fallen on the black ice lining the pavements. There was a real knack to fixing a broken wrist in an elderly patient. Often the ends of the bones were impacted and needed to be pulled apart before being realigned. I would inject local anaesthetic directly into the fracture site, feeling for the crunch of the needle into bone to know I was in the right place. Then I would lift the end of the wrist up at a ninety-degree angle to release the fracture before pulling the hand up and over to straighten it again. Sometimes the patients had paper-thin skin and if I yanked too hard there was a chance I would pull the skin off their wrists as well. Once the wrist was in the right place I'd have to keep pulling to hold it in place while a nurse put a plaster cast on to keep it in position.

Halfway through the job, I passed the first part of the MRCS exam and, to celebrate, I bought a house. After living with friends for so many years, it was such a luxury to have a kitchen and bathroom all to myself. I was no longer confined to a single room. It was also easier to shut myself away when the black clouds came. Despite the tablets, I still had waves of depression that lasted for several days. I blamed it on the shift work. I coped the only way I knew how – by ignoring text messages from friends and never answering the phone. One particularly bad weekend I heard someone knocking on my front door for ages but I stayed upstairs in bed, praying they would go away and leave me alone. My mobile started ringing so I turned it off. I just couldn't face dealing with anyone. The next weekend, when I was back to normal and out in the pub, Hannah asked me if I'd heard her knocking. Daljit had told her she was worried about me as she hadn't heard from me in days. She was on-call, so Hannah had offered to drive round and check up on me.

'I knew you were home,' she said, 'because the lights were on and your car was in the drive.'

I lied and said I must have been asleep after a night shift.

I drew the short straw to work on Millennium Eve. The registrars had come to work in black tie. By 11 p.m. we had cleared the department. Robbie Williams was blaring out on the radio and everyone was in a good mood. The IT team were hanging around in case all the computers stopped working at midnight with the Millennium Bug and we could hear the Manic Street Preachers playing at the Arms Park Stadium in the distance. Everyone went outside to watch the fireworks along with most of the junior doctors in the hospital.

Then the surgical and orthopaedic consultants on-call appeared, also in black tie. On the stroke of midnight, as we all cheered 'Happy New Year', a stream of blue lights started heading our way. Thirty seconds later the first ambulance arrived and they didn't stop. I ended up working an extra four hours just to help clear the decks for the day team.

Chapter 7

M y next post was in in colorectal surgery and it felt good to be back on the wards. I had my own house officer, Neil, who was incredibly kind with the patients and always made sure the results were checked before he went home. My registrar, Stuart, had almost finished his training. He took me under his wing and passed on all his words of wisdom. His first piece of advice was to keep my boss off the wards, out of clinic and out of theatre.

I soon fell into the routine of being an SHO, and that started in outpatients. The first patient I saw had classical symptoms of haemorrhoidal bleeding. After doing a rectal exam, I went to tell my boss what I'd found.

'Have you injected haemorrhoids before?'

'No.'

'Tell the nurse to get the trolley ready.'

He grabbed a small metal speculum called a proctoscope and pushed it into the anus, lining up the perfect view of the red, bulging haemorrhoids. Moving his head out of the way, he said, 'See those?'

'Yes.'

'Inject them at three, seven and eleven o'clock.'

The nurse passed him a syringe of five per cent phenol

with the longest needle I had ever seen screwed on the end and he slowly injected it above each pile.

I was now on my own. I tried to hide my nerves from the next patient I saw. I didn't want them to know I'd never done it before. I pushed the proctoscope in and lined it up so I could see the piles. I grasped the syringe from the nurse and with a shaking hand I pierced the anal mucosa. The patient shot out his legs with a loud scream, nearly kicking me in the face. The nurse caught the syringe as I ducked.

'Everything all right . . . ?'

Stuart had come to save the day. As he took over, he said to the patient, 'It can be painful when they're large.' He whispered to me, 'Can you see that pale white line?'

'Yes.'

'That's the dentate line. They can't feel anything if you inject above it. You've just seen what happens if you don't.'

I never made that mistake again.

Clinics weren't the only place that I looked up people's bottoms. As the surgical SHO on-call I was guardian of the rectal trolley with all the kit I needed to assess patients on the wards. The first time I had to use it was in the middle of the night. I'd been asked to see an old man with a pseudo-obstruction. His bowel had stopped working because of his other medical problems, leaving him with a painful distended abdomen full of gas. It was stopping him breathing properly and it was my job to deflate him using a sigmoidoscope. It was a twenty-five-centimetre-long tube that could look further into the rectum. It had a blunt probe to push it into the anal canal. Once that was removed, a light source was attached and a hand pump blew air down the scope, forcing the bowel walls to open up, giving a clear view to safely push the scope in further. But instead of a nice, bright clinic room, I was now on a ward in the dark with a nurse holding a torch so I could see what I was doing. I switched on the bedside light and gently shook the patient awake.

'I've come to try and get rid of the gas in your tummy. I need you to roll over on to your side and pull your pyjama bottoms down to your knees.'

I pulled his bottom towards me so it lay on the edge of the bed and put a large white pad underneath him, followed by a dollop of K-Y jelly to help the scope go in. I plugged in the light source and got down on my knees. After pushing in the first part of the tube, I pulled out the probe and put it on the pad beside me, except it slipped and fell, hitting my knee on its way to the floor, leaving a smear of stool on my scrubs.

As I leaned closer to look down the scope, a lock of hair that I'd carefully tucked behind my ears fell forwards and landed in the jelly. As I wiggled the scope back and forth my head slipped and my nose touched his bottom. I kept inflating with air to try to open up the bowel so I could push the scope in further but my hands were slick with the lube and I lost my grip. The scope fell out, accompanied by a huge fart, a torrent of liquid shit and a sigh of relief from the patient. I grabbed a kidney dish to try to catch the rest. I felt a cold, wet patch on my waist and knew I was covered in it. My bleep went off.

'Sorry. I've got to get this.'

I packed up the trolley and rushed to theatres for a

new set of scrubs, leaving the poor nurse to clean up the mess.

Another glamorous on-call job was performing a manual evacuation. When someone was so constipated that their rectum was full and they couldn't push it out, it was my job to remove it with my hands. The first time I did it was on an inmate from the local prison. The rumour on the wards was that he'd murdered three women. He had a straggly black beard and was covered in tattoos. There were two policemen who stayed with him at all times, and it took a bit of juggling to work out how to get him in position and still keep him handcuffed to the bed. He was so constipated that I had to reach in up to my elbow to scoop out the thick, black, tarry stool. I filled half a yellow clinical waste bag with shit.

One day, Stuart decided to play a practical joke on Neil, who was about to move to another firm. Stuart thought it would be funny to wind him up. He bleeped him and said, 'There's a patient on the ward who needs a manual evac. Liz can't do it as I need her in theatre but she'll tell you what to do.'

Neil was a nervous wreck when I found him on the wards.

'Right,' I said. 'You need to change into scrubs. Go via the canteen on your way and pick up a knickerbocker glory spoon to help you scoop it out. Cover your hands with Hibiscrub before putting on your gloves. It helps with the smell afterwards. You'll need lots of K-Y jelly, and make sure your nails don't pierce the gloves. See you later and good luck.'

The nurse on the ward was in on it too, playing along

and confirming that, yes, the patient did need it doing. I saw Neil go off to the canteen to get the spoon while I went to find Stuart in the mess but we lost track of time.

'No!' said Stuart suddenly, 'we forgot to tell Neil it was a wind-up.'

I rushed to the ward to find him gowned and gloved about to go into the patient's room with an auxiliary nurse as a chaperone. Our nurse had gone on her break.

'Neil! Stop! It's a joke. He doesn't need it doing.'

'Why, you little shit!'

The coffee and cake was on Stuart for the rest of his time on the firm.

Although I saw a lot of literal shit on-call, there was very little during the elective cancer operations because the patients were cleaned out first. They came in two days beforehand for bowel prep, which involved drinking six litres of something that looked like Fairy Liquid before spending the next forty-eight hours on the commode. I felt so sorry for them as I prescribed it, thankful that I didn't have to drink it myself.

In theatre, it was my job to stand between the patient's legs holding a large metal retractor. It had a small lip to keep the bowel underneath it in place. I hated holding it because I couldn't see anything. Whenever I did stand on my tiptoes to peek over, the retractor would slip and I'd get bombarded by a torrent of swear words. Another downside of standing between the legs was that I got to see if my bowel prep had worked. If the patient hadn't completely emptied their bowels before getting on the table, I'd end up with a puddle around my feet.

When I did get to see what was going on inside, I was

no longer fascinated by the wriggling of the small bowel. I was too busy trying to memorise the mechanics of surgery. There were so many questions running through my head. What were the names of all the different instruments? Why were different sutures used for bowel, blood vessels and skin? The answers weren't found in a textbook. It was all learned on the job.

As part of my training, I had to go on a Basic Surgical Skills course. The first day was spent learning how to tie a surgical knot. It was simply three throws of a reef knot. Right over left, left over right, each throw lying neatly on top of the last. It was easy to do when suturing skin as I could use both hands, but deep inside the abdomen, knots were always tied with the non-dominant hand. While my right hand kept hold of the long end of the suture, I had to learn to flick and throw the short end with my left to create each knot. Once I'd mastered that, the next skill was to tie one at depth. Instead of using both hands to tighten the knot, it had to be snugged down using one finger. If I pulled up on the long end of the suture to help me, it could rip the blood vessel being tied off, causing more bleeding. It was a lot harder than it looked.

Two days later I was back in theatre and desperate to show off my new skills. However, tying knots with bare hands while gossiping with friends on a course was very different to tying knots wearing gloves slippery with abdominal fat when Stuart was in a hurry and my knots had to hold. Feeling flat, I took a couple of packs of ties and some spare gloves back to my on-call room and spent the night throwing endless knots around my big toe.

I was back in theatre the next day. Stuart had to leave

to see a sick patient on the ward. My boss had resected – cut out – a tumour and needed to join the bowel back together. That normally meant passing lots of sutures through both bowel ends, which I held on to before passing them in turn to Stuart to tie. But there was no Stuart, and my boss was too impatient to tie the knots himself. Time to see if my late-night practice had been worth it. Muscle memory took over and I went into autopilot.

'Well done,' said my boss.

Praise was hard to come by, so those two words meant so much.

After a few months I was beginning to feel a lot more confident managing surgical patients, and Stuart would often let me decide when patients were ready to go home. One Monday morning we'd trawled the length and breadth of the hospital seeing the patients from the weekend take. There was one more medical outlier left on the geriatric ward, right at the other end of the hospital. It was a good half-a-mile walk to see her. Stuart and I looked at each other. She'd been fine the day before and we both had work to do before the afternoon clinic. Lunch was calling. I said that I'd go back and check on her later.

Just as I turned to head for the mess, my boss came on to the corridor.

'Everything OK?'

'Yes. No problems.'

'How's the lady on F8?'

Bluffing, I said, 'Better. She might be going home later.'

'Carry on.'

As soon as he turned the corner, I started running to

the ward. I pushed open the door to her room, but there was a different woman inside. I found one of the doctors at the nursing station and asked him where she was.

'She had a massive rectal bleed in the night. I spoke to the consultant on-call but he said she wouldn't survive an operation so we kept her comfortable and she died early this morning.'

The consultant on-call was our boss. He knew I'd lied to him. He never mentioned it and I never said anything but the lesson was learned. Never lie. The boss always knows.

I actually enjoyed looking up people's bottoms and loved the variety that colorectal surgery offered. As well as the large cancer resections there was fine anal work repairing fissures and fistulas. Because I was working more regular hours I was sleeping better and no longer spent the weekends in bed. It also meant I could see more of my friends and I now looked forward to drunken nights out when I could let my hair down and remember how to enjoy myself outside of work.

Back in theatre, I had moved on to the next stage of my training – how to use the instruments. Like a magician learning sleight of hand, there were three key skills I had to master. The first was palming. I had to be able to suture while holding a pair of scissors in the same hand. It reduced the number of times the scrub nurse had to pass me things and it helped the operation go smoothly. I spent hours practising with spare instruments as I flipped the scissors up and down across my palm.

Then it was on to the back-hand. Needles should always enter tissue at a ninety-degree angle to make the smallest possible hole. It was easy when stitching towards myself, but I couldn't go the other way without poking Stuart with my elbow. By reversing the angle of the needle and my wrist, I could keep my elbows down and it was quicker to close a wound.

Finally, I had to learn to cut sutures with my left hand since my right was often holding a retractor and it was clumsy when I had to put it down to pick up the scissors. The trick was to push down with my thumb instead of pulling up with my fingers. The one thing I couldn't manage, though, was cutting sutures to the right length. They were always too long or too short and the consultant would often have to trim them again. He finally let me in on the secret. 'It's one of the rules of surgery. The ends are never the right length unless you're the consultant. You'll say it to your own trainees one day.'

I hoped he was right.

Chapter 8

My next job was in trauma and orthopaedics, and I was completely out of my depth from the start. In A&E I knew which fractures needed to be admitted, but now I was the one looking after the patients, I had no idea how to manage them. I was working for five consultants and no longer had a house officer. I was so busy chasing blood results and X-rays of the fifty or so patients in my care that I thought I would never get to theatre. I was expected to drop everything whenever a consultant decided to grace us with his presence for an impromptu ward round.

Every morning started with a trauma meeting where the new cases were presented, and I learned a whole new language. It wasn't good enough to describe a broken ankle as a fractured tibia. I had to say whether the break was complete or incomplete, if it was oblique, spiral, transverse or comminuted, whether there was angulation, rotation, distraction or impaction and if the joint was involved. I quickly realised this would make my life a lot easier when discussing cases with the registrar over the phone, when they couldn't see the films.

———

The first time I presented a case on a ward round I started describing the patient's medical problems when my registrar, Dylan, muttered in my ear, 'Show them the X-ray.'

I was so used to working in general surgery that I'd forgotten this was orthopaedics. All they wanted to see was how the bones looked after the fracture had been fixed. It was my job to look after everything else. A lot of my patients were in their seventies and eighties and had fallen and broken their hips, but it was their bronchitis and angina stopping them from going home. Thankfully, there was a geriatric consultant assigned to the orthopaedic wards to help me look after everything but the bones.

I thought the on-calls would be easy but I was wrong. I was constantly on the phone to the registrars, asking them what to do with the patients, until I learned the ropes. It was nice to be back in A&E, though, and I spent many an hour covered in warm plaster of Paris as I straightened a footballer's broken leg. When I wasn't doing that, I was dealing with rugby players' dislocated shoulders. The men normally took one look at me and thought I'd never be strong enough, which worked to my advantage. They weren't expecting a struggle so they started to relax and it was normally fairly easy to manipulate the shoulder into place. Occasionally, though, brute force was needed. I'd have to hike up my skirt, put a gloved foot in their armpit to act as a lever and pull on their hand with all my might to try to bring the shoulder back.

There was one Tuesday shift that was particularly quiet and I used the opportunity to go to theatre and watch Dylan do the trauma list. The first patient on the list had a fractured hip. Instead of green drapes, Dylan stuck a large plastic sheet with a huge pocket to the patient's skin.

'What's that for?'

'To collect the blood.'

He slashed the thigh open straight down to the bone and used a large retractor to keep the muscles back, ignoring the bleeding. I was desperate to get the diathermy forceps and buzz the veins. The nurse opened trays of what looked like Meccano. After taking an X-ray on the table, Dylan chose a metal plate and some screws and started drilling it to the femur. It seemed so brutal. Even the skin wound was closed with large bites of thread. Nothing about this operation appealed to me.

It wasn't all hammers and drills, though. One day after the morning trauma meeting, one of the consultants came up to me and asked, 'Who taught you to plait your hair?'

'My mum.'

'Come to theatre with me this afternoon.'

He was doing a repair to an anterior cruciate ligament. This is one of two tendons that pass through the middle of the knee to stop it wobbling when you walk, and was often torn in bad football tackles. He'd already started by the time I was scrubbed.

'I've been learning to plait too.'

He'd taken one of the accessory hamstring tendons from the back of the leg and was making a four-stranded braid to replace the damaged tendon in the knee.

'A hairdresser showed me how to do this. It makes the new tendon much stronger before I screw it into place.'

Every Friday morning there was a large fracture clinic

when the team would see over a hundred patients who'd broken their fingers, hands and wrists in the previous week. At eleven o'clock on the dot, everyone in clinic, including the nurses, stopped for coffee. I was expected to come even if I was busy on the wards. The first time I was summoned I was pissed off because I had a long list of things to do. And then I walked into the coffee room and saw the pile of hot bacon sandwiches and doughnuts that had been made by the canteen just for us. The consultant had a standing arrangement and paid for everything. For fifteen minutes we would chat about how the week had gone and what we were going to do at the weekend. It was a wonderful moment of stillness among the chaos of the wards and it meant we always ended the week on a high.

After six months of orthopaedics, I was ready to move on. I was glad that I'd done the job because it would help me pass that part of my exam, but it hadn't been a happy time. It wasn't just that I was back to being a house officer again or that I didn't like the operating. It was because I was the only woman in a man's world. All the other surgeons were men. Most of them were well behaved. Coffee room conversation often concerned rugby, sharing crude jokes or bragging about their latest sexual conquests. Every once in a while a wandering hand would stray in my direction.

I could see that if I didn't join in with the banter, I'd risk being called a prude. I was also aware that I was missing out on whatever was said between bosses and trainees in the changing rooms and could feel the shift in conversation whenever they saw me in the coffee room. Something had to change. Now, whenever someone told a rude joke, I told a dirtier one. I started drinking pints of lager instead of gin and tonic in the Philly. I hinted at a fictitious sex life and eventually was seen as one of the lads. Although I hated myself, I thought it was worth it to feel part of the team. It made me feel less vulnerable. By learning to play that character I was no longer a target for innuendo or any sexual advances. I felt sorry for the women who would follow in my footsteps and have to go through the same sort of experience, but I just wasn't strong enough to speak up. Besides, I needed a good reference to help me get my next job. It was just another role to play in the theatre of surgery.

Chapter 9

My next post was in urology and I was looking forward to a fresh start in a new hospital a little
further afield. On the first day, I'd given myself plenty of
time to get there but it wasn't enough. The traffic was
awful and I was now running late. I rushed on to the
ward and blurted at the nurse standing behind the desk,
'I'm Liz Ball, the new urology SHO. Has the ward
round started yet?'

He burst out laughing. 'Dr Dick and Dr Ball! You
couldn't make this up.'

Confused, I looked past him at the other SHO who'd
been waiting for me.

'Hi. I'm Richard.'

The two consultants and our new registrar arrived to
start the round. They also thought this was hilarious, and
by the end of the morning, I'd been christened 'Tess'. As
in testicle. It seemed to be automatically assumed that I
would be OK with this. Tess would stick for the next
two years in that hospital.

I had my own patients to see in clinic again and it was
good to feel useful. Instead of plaster casts and X-rays, my
days were spent handling male genitalia. It took a few

days to get over my embarrassment and my surname didn't help. I'd been given some simple cases to break me in gently, harmless lumps and bumps. The nurse brought the first patient through.

'Hi. I'm Dr Ball. I gather you've found a lump in your testicle.'

'Is that really your name?'

'Yes. It really is.'

I introduced myself as Liz after that.

Once a month I was sent off to do a solo outreach clinic in Caerphilly. The outpatient department was tiny and there was barely space for the examination couch in my clinic room. The first time was nerve-wracking as there was no consultant to ask for help. The nurse brought in the pile of notes for the patients booked that morning. I scanned the first referral letter. It was a man in his seventies with difficulty peeing.

'Could you get the first patient for me?'

'Of course, doctor. Cup of tea?'

'Yes please.'

She went off to get him. There was a knock on the door. I turned in my chair, reaching out to take the cup of tea from her. Instead, I found myself holding the penis of my first patient. I'm not sure who blushed more, him or me. By the end of the clinic I'd realised that it was common for the men to get straight to the point, dropping their trousers and pants as soon as they entered the room.

I also covered the erectile dysfunction clinic. First, I had to learn the local Welsh euphemisms. Half-mast or full mast? Do you get a morning glory? What's the angle of the dangle? Once I'd worked out what their erection was like, if they could get one in the first place, I could then do something about it. If they had a medical problem like diabetes that stopped them getting hard, I could prescribe Viagra. The others had a choice of a penis pump to get the blood flowing or pushing a small wax pellet down their urethra. When the wax melted, the drug inside was released and would produce an erection. It was my job to show them how to melt the pellet by rubbing my hands around my imaginary penis to warm it. I must have missed that lecture in medical school.

I also saw a lot of women with urinary incontinence, and one of my bosses took a special interest in this; a new procedure had just been developed using a mesh to solve the problem. He showed me how to assess the patients in clinic to see how bad their incontinence was. After doing a pelvic exam on one woman to assess her muscle tone, he asked her to cough.

'But if I cough, I'll wet myself,' she said.

'I know it's a bit embarrassing,' he said, 'but I need to see how bad the problem is.'

The nurse put an absorbent pad between the woman's knees. I didn't know where to look. She coughed and a spurt of urine came out. I could see her blushing as the nurse went to help her get dressed.

One month later the woman was on her way to theatre to have the new procedure. My boss had invited another surgeon to show him how to do it. A rep from the company who sold the mesh had also come along to watch. It was going to be crowded. The anaesthetist pushed the patient into the operating room and I was shocked to see that she was still awake. This operation was being done using a spinal anaesthetic. I felt so sorry for her with all these men watching. Once he'd inserted the mesh to create a sling under her urethra, the visiting surgeon told my boss to ask her to cough. This was how you knew whether the sling was tight enough.

In front of a room full of strangers, she did as he asked and a squirt of urine shot out, almost hitting him in the eye. Thank God her face was hidden from the men she was peeing in front of by a sterile screen. My boss pulled the mesh a bit tighter and asked her to cough again. This went on and on until finally the mesh was tight enough and he could fix it in place. I could feel her embarrassment behind the screen and felt so uncomfortable. I never wanted to see anything like that again.

Halfway through the job, a urologist hit the national papers for removing the wrong kidney and it shook us all up. It was what is known in medicine as a 'never event'. It should be impossible for it to happen, but a series of tiny errors meant that it did. The next week I had to look after three men who were all coming in to have their kidney tumours removed. They were all in the same four-bedded bay. Two were left-sided and one was on the right. Two were called David Matthews and the other was Matthew Davies. I spent that week double- and triple-checking everything and even got the men to write on themselves with a black marker pen to confirm which kidney was coming out.

Although I liked the variety of the surgery and the fun I had in clinics, urology wasn't for me. I wanted more sewing and cutting and less urine. It also wasn't great for my social life. On the rare occasion that I did meet someone I fancied in a bar, the conversation would inevitably end in the same way.

'So, what do you do?'

'I'm a doctor.'

'What kind of doctor?'

'A urologist.'

'What does that mean?'

'I spend my days looking at penises.'

Exit stage left. I never found a man who was willing to risk his penis being compared to those I saw in my day job. Time to move on to more familiar territory, back to the comfort of general surgery.

Chapter 10

For my final year as an SHO I was back doing colorectal surgery again and I was looking forward to it. I knew how to handle post-op patients on the ward and what to do in clinic, and hoped I could build on the surgical skills I'd learned the year before. My registrar, Mike, was always laughing and joking and we got on like a house on fire. I knew this was going to be a good year.

As well as the main colorectal clinics, I had to do an outreach clinic in a tiny cottage hospital in the Welsh valleys. I went with my boss while Mike stayed behind to do an endoscopy list. I loved it there. I had my own nurse, Chris, who quickly became my second mum. She always made sure there was a cup of tea and a plate of hot buttered toast waiting for me. The clinic was a mixture of colorectal and general surgical patients. The lumps and bumps, hernias and varicose veins were a welcome distraction from the endless haemorrhoids as well as being good revision practice for my upcoming exams.

I also got to do a bit more in theatre. I started to learn how to free up the colon and join it back together and I mastered how to repair inguinal hernias. I did a lot of them under local anaesthetic. It was great for the patients because they could go home a few hours later instead of having to stay overnight. It also refined my surgical skills. I had to learn to be a lot more delicate as the patients could feel any pushing and pulling. It also meant changing how I asked for instruments. Knife, blade and needle aren't the best words to use when a patient can hear. We developed our own sign language instead.

One day, as a treat, I was given my own local hernia list when my boss was away at a conference. I went on to the ward to do the pre-op checks with a few medical students who were tagging along, hoping they'd be able to practise examining the hernias once I'd left. After consenting my first patient, he looked at me and said, 'Thank you, nurse,' before asking the tall male student beside me how long the operation would take.

The list was going smoothly and I was running on time. My last patient had a huge hernia extending down into his scrotum and he wasn't fit for a haircut as his heart valve disease meant that a general anaesthetic might kill him. I cut down through the layers of tissue and had just opened the hernia sac when he coughed and three feet of small bowel whooshed out of his abdomen towards the floor. He tried to sit up. I put my hands on his chest.

'Stay where you are.' I looked at the nurse. 'Call Mike. Get an anaesthetist. Open a major tray.'

Mike stuck his head through the door. 'What the hell's going on?'

I jerked my head towards the patient and whispered, 'He's awake.'

'Ah. OK.' Mike leaned over the patient and said, 'Hi

there. We're going to have to put you to sleep to fix the hernia. It's a bit bigger than we thought.'

The on-call anaesthetist arrived, took one look at the bowel hanging out and rolled her eyes.

'He's got a tight aortic stenosis,' I said. 'That's why I was doing it under local.'

She flicked through his notes and asked the theatre assistant to draw up the necessary drugs. As Mike went to get scrubbed, I prepped and draped the skin again after sloshing disinfectant over the hanging loops of bowel.

'Who put him on this list?'

'I'm not sure,' I said.

'You never do a hernia this big under local. Small ones only. Otherwise this is what happens. Jesus Christ.'

Mike looked at the anaesthetist. 'How is he?'

'Fine at the moment. No thanks to Miss Ball, here.'

The patient left hospital a few days later, just before my boss came back.

I had my fair share of excitement during the on-calls as well, including my first ever stabbing. I was already in A&E with Mike, seeing a drug addict with a groin abscess, when the paramedics burst through the doors, shouting, 'We're losing him!'

A young man had been stabbed in his right upper quadrant, the part of the abdomen that contains the liver, gallbladder and part of the large intestine, and blood was oozing from the wound pads strapped to his stomach. Mike rang theatres. 'There's a stabbing in resus. We're coming up now.'

While he was on the phone to the consultant, the patient arrested. The only way to stop the bleeding was an immediate operation. I started doing CPR while the anaesthetist intubated him. A nurse took over while I got a chair to stand on. I climbed on to the trolley, straddled the patient and started doing chest compressions again. We were pushed along the corridor at lightning speed with the anaesthetist running alongside us. Theatres were waiting. The scrub nurse was already gowned and gloved, checking her trays of instruments. I clambered off while the anaesthetic SHO took over and I went to get scrubbed. Mike was amazing. He put a clamp on the aorta to slow down the bleeding and stuffed the abdomen with gauze packs to soak up the blood. By some miracle the heart restarted. We stood back to catch our breath while the anaesthetists resuscitated him.

As Mike slowly removed the packs, I filled bowl after bowl with thick clots of blood. There was a huge gash in the young man's liver. I was trying to remember my anatomy to work out how to repair it when Mike asked for more large packs.

'Packs?'

'Yes. I'm going to sandwich the liver between them to compress it until the bleeding stops.'

'Then what?'

'ITU. If he makes it through the night, he'll go to the liver unit in Birmingham.'

'Oh.' I was gutted that I wouldn't be seeing major surgery.

'We can't fix him now. He's too unstable. Damage limitation, remember. Stop the bleeding. Warm him up. Fill him up. Only then do you go back for a second look.'

A few months later I got called at 11 p.m. on a Sunday

night. It had been an awful weekend. I'd had very little sleep and was ready to drop. I went to A&E to see an elderly man with peritonitis. He was pale, cold and clammy with a racing pulse. His abdomen was distended and exquisitely tender to touch. The chest X-ray showed free air under his diaphragm. It was almost certainly a perforated colon and he needed to go straight to theatre.

I rang Mike but he was dealing with an emergency on the wards so I had to call the consultant. Luckily, he was still in the hospital doing paperwork and agreed to meet me in the scrub room. I stood next to him as we unwrapped our gowns.

'Put a plastic apron on first,' he said. 'Wear two pairs of gloves. Put a thick layer of Hibiscrub between each pair. Trust me.'

I did what he said. As a reward for working so hard all weekend, he let me open the abdomen. This was huge for me; I spent most of my time in theatre assisting the registrars, who wanted to get all the cutting in they could before they became consultants. Opening a distended abdomen is difficult to say the least. Everything is under tension. Skin, fascia and muscle are stretched to bursting point and one false move could mean I cut directly into the bowel without realising it. I stroked the scalpel through the skin, millimetre by millimetre, hoping to stop just before I punctured the peritoneum.

However, the skin was so thin that my blade went straight into the abdominal cavity, releasing a torrent of liquid shit. A thick chocolate milkshake shot straight up to the ceiling, covering the lights before dripping back down on to the table and me. The consultant had stepped back, knowing what was going to happen. With a wicked glint in his eye, he said, 'Welcome to the club. Your hands are going to smell like shit for the next two weeks. Everything you eat will smell like shit as well. Aren't you glad you're a surgeon?'

But I was, despite the mess I was in. The man turned out to have bowel cancer that had caused a complete blockage leading to a perforation upstream as the pressure from above caused his colon to burst. Because the abdominal cavity was contaminated with faeces, it wasn't safe to excise the cancer and join the ends together. The consultant stapled off the distal end of the colon, leaving a stump. The proximal end would have to be brought through a hole in the abdominal wall to form a colostomy. I got to help the consultant remove the cancer and bring out a stoma instead of being stuck between the legs missing out on what was happening. I was as happy as a pig in shit, despite being covered in it.

Once I'd passed my MRCS exam and could call myself Miss Ball, all my thoughts were focused on how to be a registrar. I paid close attention to everything Mike did, conscious that I would be in his shoes in six months' time. One weekend I'd admitted ten women all in their sixties with left-sided abdominal pain. I couldn't separate them in my head and on the morning ward round I kept mixing them up. Mike took over and presented them flawlessly. He was like a machine. Once the round was done, I asked him how he did it. He said it had taken him years of practice. 'It won't click until you're the one deciding whether to take a patient to theatre in the middle of the night. It's only then that the details start to stick.'

Halfway through the job there was a change in the junior doctors' contract that meant the house officers had to stop working at 10 p.m. and I now had to cover the wards as well as the new admissions and theatres. Two weeks after this was introduced, I was on nights with a house officer called Nia. She was planning to be a GP despite me doing my best to persuade her to switch to surgery but she was great to work with as she always made sure the ward jobs were done before she went to bed. A local cottage hospital called to say they were sending over a woman with a rectal bleed. I looked at my watch. It had just gone ten. No point going to bed. I started updating the handover list for the morning when the patient arrived. The nurse and I looked at her.

The woman was as white as the sheet she was lying on apart from the four litres of fresh blood clot between her legs. Her pulse was weak and thready and she was groaning in pain.

'What are her obs?'

'I can't get a blood pressure.'

'Get me a bloods trolley and fluids now,' I said. 'Bleep Nia. She needs to see this.'

Nia stumbled on to the ward. Before she could speak, I said, 'Put in two large venflons and take bloods for cross-matching. Ring the labs and ask for two units of O neg, then squeeze through a bag of fluid stat.'

I turned to the nurses and asked them to put in a catheter and get an ECG. Her pulse and blood pressure had picked up a little with the fluid and I scanned through the note sent over with her. It didn't tell me anything useful and my patient could barely talk.

I rang the registrar on for the night and he told me he was on his way. By the time he arrived, the first unit of blood was going in and there was a bit of colour in her cheeks. It was now 1 a.m. She still had low abdominal pain but there was no more rectal bleeding and her pulse and blood pressure were stable. He suggested topping her up overnight with blood and platelets and teeing her up for a colonoscopy in the morning.

I apologised to Nia for getting her out of bed. 'I thought you needed to see how to manage a sick patient.'

'How do you stay so calm? I would have been a total wreck.'

'I used to panic too, but I realised that made the nurses panic and nothing got done.' I told her that I learned to cope by giving the team jobs to do while I worked through the basics – airway, breathing, circulation. It gave me time to think what to do next. 'Inside my head I'm freaking out, but I can't show it. I call it internal brown trousers, external calm.'

The hospital had a good reputation for training and I loved teaching the medical students on the wards. The firm do was the highlight of each five-week block and I lost count of the number of pretty girls who'd laughed charmingly at everything a consultant said, hoping it would help them get a job. In some hospitals this actually worked. I remember hearing on the grapevine how one of the consultants had dumped a pile of CVs on their SHO's lap and said, 'Pick out the pretty blonde ones for me to interview as my next house officer.'

Flirting was common, especially around the operating

table. Most of the time it was fun and a way to break the tension or pass the time, but it could easily go too far. As the only woman on the team, pressed up close to my male colleagues with only thin cotton scrubs between us, it was hard to say when a line had been crossed. I resorted to becoming one of the lads again to make sure I wasn't seen as 'mistress' material.

One night after a firm do, we'd all gone on to the local nightclub. I was dancing with Mike and some of the nurses when a consultant from another firm came up to join us. The music switched to a slow song and he asked me to dance. I couldn't say no. He pulled me in closer and I could feel his erection pressing against me. He leaned in for a snog but I pushed him away.

'Come on. It's just a kiss. It's only cheating if we go to a dark corner.'

I lied about having a boyfriend and ran off to the toilets. Later he got off with one of the nurses. It was never mentioned again.

After almost eighteen months of colorectal surgery, I was seriously considering it as a career. I'd managed to get study leave to go on a course for future colorectal trainees. I finally felt like a grown-up as I sat in a lecture theatre with my peers, all ready to start the next phase of their surgical training. It was fascinating hearing what the latest developments were and learning different ways to treat anal fissures and abscesses. But it was the opening keynote that blew my mind. The professor giving the lecture told us that the rectum is the most sensitive part of the human body because it can differentiate between solid, liquid and gas. The whole room was silent while we processed that thought. He went on to say that every one of us knew what was going to come out of our anus when we relaxed the sphincter – poo, diarrhoea or a fart. A ripple of laughter went around the room as we realised he was right. It made me love colorectal surgery even more.

The end of my rotation was now fast approaching and I didn't have a registrar job lined up. I'd sent off several application forms but wasn't getting shortlisted. It was a box-ticking exercise and I simply didn't have enough research on my CV. The successful applicants had taken time out to do an MD or a PhD and I couldn't compete with the three papers I'd had published. I was starting to get scared about my future as I had a mortgage to pay and had no idea how to make ends meet if I didn't get a job.

Time was running out when I saw an advert for a PhD in thyroid cancer. Three years was a long time away from surgery. There was no on-call and it would mean a large drop in salary, but I had enough to keep a roof over my head and it meant I could stay in Cardiff with my friends.

Now the pressure was off, I agreed to go on a last-minute skiing holiday with Daljit. I was terrible at skiing but loved the après-ski and was sad to come home. The next weekend, Daljit asked me to come over. When she answered the door, she had an odd look on her face. I followed her into the lounge and sat down.

'I need to tell you something,' she said.

'What's up?'

'I think you might have a drinking problem.'

'Me?'

There was a long silence.

'You don't remember, do you?'

'Remember what?'

'Talking to Aidan.'

'About what?'

'You said he looked like a paedophile because of his moustache.'

'I'd never say anything like that.'

'You did. And then you went back to the bar as if nothing had happened.'

'Shit.'

'I think you need help.'

'Don't be silly. I just had too much to drink. It was the last night of the holiday. It won't happen again.'

'It's not just that. There are days when no one can get hold of you. I know you get down sometimes. I'm worried you might have bipolar disorder.'

I didn't know what to say. I kept staring at the floor, letting it all sink in. Tears started to fall, and she put her arm around me for a hug. I turned to look at her and saw she was crying too.

'What do I do?'

We spent the rest of the afternoon slowly piecing together what had happened to me over the last few years. I could see that my drinking had got out of hand. I tried to justify it as a way to fit in with the men I worked with, but it was more than that. I didn't know when to stop. I loved the confidence that alcohol gave me. I was popular when I was drunk. I was liked. It made me feel invincible. But I was obviously hurting a lot of people and that was hard to take.

I asked her how long she'd known about my depression. She said she'd always known. I thought I'd done a pretty good job of covering it. Surgery had been excellent training. I was so used to acting on the wards to fit in with my male peers, I simply carried on outside of work. It was just another mask to help me hide what I was actually feeling from people who loved me.

I admitted that I was also worried about money. In the last couple of months, I'd stopped opening my credit card bills, scared of how much I owed. I'd been spending money I didn't have on things I didn't need. The most dangerous time was just after a run of night shifts had ended and I was almost euphoric with lack of sleep. I would scour the internet trying to stay awake and then a few days later, parcels would arrive that I couldn't remember ordering.

Maybe I did have bipolar disorder. That terrified me. A mental illness might stop me from becoming a surgeon or, worse still, being a doctor at all. I tried to tell her that I couldn't see anyone, fearful of what a diagnosis would mean. It was hard enough coping in surgery as a woman, but with a mental illness on top? I couldn't go there. She told me not to worry about that yet. What was more important was getting help, and we'd sort the rest out later.

'You need to see your GP. I can go with you, if you like.'

'No. It's OK. I'll be fine.'

I needed to be by myself to take it all in. She gave me another huge hug before I left, and I promised to text her in the morning once I'd made the appointment.

The GP referred me to see a community psychiatrist.

I felt so ashamed as I sat in the waiting room. By the time I was called through, the chair I'd been sitting on was soaked with sweat. It was my first time being a real patient. I could remember from medical school how to take a psychiatric history and how a patient's appearance and body language were taken into account. I looked down at what I was wearing, wondering if I'd worn the right clothes. He told me to try to forget I was a doctor, and just answer his questions without thinking too much.

At the end of the consultation, he said I didn't have bipolar disorder but something called cyclothymia, a mental disorder causing frequent mood swings from depression to hypomania. He also said that it might be the Seroxat antidepressants that were causing the manic episodes.

Now I officially had a mental illness, I was scared. I asked him what it would mean for my career. He couldn't say, but he hoped things would improve once I stopped the tablets. He warned me that coming off them would be horrible – the withdrawal symptoms had been likened to drug addicts getting clean – and that it would take six months in total to slowly wean myself off, a quarter of a tablet at a time. I was grateful I was just about to start my PhD and would have no clinical commitments or patients to look after. I just hoped it worked and the Liz my friends knew and loved would return.

Chapter 11

I was going to spend the next four years investigating what makes a slow-growing thyroid cancer suddenly become aggressive and kill within months. The bulk of my work involved cutting wafer-thin slices from wax blocks of thyroid tissue, staining them to identify target proteins and then counting the positive cells down a microscope. I swapped my suits and heels for jeans and trainers, and my scalpel and retractor for microtomes and pipettes. It was hard at first because I didn't have a timetable to follow. It was up to me what hours I worked. All that mattered was having something to present at the monthly departmental meetings.

I loved having the freedom to think and work when I wanted to, instead of when I had to. Everyone stopped for coffee and lunch breaks and it was so refreshing not having to talk about medicine all the time. I realised how boring my life had been when all I did was work, drink, eat and sleep. One of the lab techs showed me how to do the *Telegraph* cryptic crossword and it became our lunchtime ritual. I lived in hope that one day I would complete it without having to cheat and use my phone to solve the anagrams. I slowly weaned myself off the antidepressants and started to feel like my old self again.

After the first year, I managed to get some locum work as an A&E registrar to top up my salary. My first shift was at the minor injury unit in Neath. It was meant to be quiet because all the major emergencies were taken straight to Swansea. Most of the things I saw were fairly straightforward – the usual cuts, sprains and fractures. One night an elderly man came in with a supra-pubic catheter that needed changing. He was bypassing urine around the hole in his abdomen and his trousers were soaked. It was normally a very quick procedure – deflate the balloon of water keeping it in the bladder, pull the catheter out and replace it with a new one. This time, however, the catheter was stuck. I pulled and pulled but it wouldn't budge. After double-checking the balloon was definitely empty, I gave it one final heave. The catheter came out along with a glob of grey gunk that went straight into my open mouth. I gagged, sticking my tongue out to stop me swallowing it. As soon as I'd put the new catheter in, I ran to the toilet to scrape my tongue clean.

The work in Neath dried up so I moved further afield to Bristol. I planned to work Wednesday, Thursday and Friday nights once a month. I'd hoped I'd be able to get a few hours' sleep like I'd done in Neath so I'd have the energy to stain slides in the day, but the unit was always busy. Friends at work were starting to notice that I was nodding off at lunchtime and I realised it wasn't sustainable. I told the locum agency that I'd be stopping at the end of the month.

On my final shift I'd almost cleared the waiting room

when the bat phone went to let us know about a multi-car pile-up. A car had pulled out at a junction hitting a minivan full of men on their way home after a stag do. The man driving the car was way over the limit and had died at the scene. The van driver and the passengers were heading our way, all with potentially serious injuries. Between majors and resus there were only eight beds, and four of them were already occupied. The trauma team arrived and we didn't have long to wait.

The van driver went straight to resus. Blood was pouring from his nose and mouth. He had two black eyes from where he'd hit the steering wheel. The anaesthetist put an oxygen mask on his face but couldn't get a good seal. 'I can feel his face moving.'

I had a closer look. The driver had broken both the upper and lower jaw bones on each side, which meant his face was disconnected from the rest of his skull. If I didn't stop the bleeding, the blood from his nose would go into his lungs. I pushed in some nasal packs but they didn't work. One of the nurses got the ENT registrar on the phone.

'I'm on my way, but in the meantime put two large urinary catheters down each nostril, inflate the balloons and pull up on them. The pressure should stop the bleeding as it lifts the facial bones into the right position.'

It worked. I got one of the nurses to hold on to the catheters while I looked at his X-rays. He had a widened mediastinum, a large haemothorax and a dislocated right hip. His abdomen was tender to touch and there was blood coming out of the catheter bag. The surgical registrar prepped to put in a chest drain while I wrote up blood and fluids before being dragged to see the sickest of the passengers.

I thought he'd ruptured his spleen, and after referring him to the surgeons I was about to move on to the next man when I got pulled to see a nineteen-year-old boy with asthma who couldn't breathe. I listened to his chest. Nothing. Just like the taxi driver I'd seen as a house officer. I asked for some urgent nebulisers and steroids and got the nurse to bleep the medical registrar. I was now losing the plot. There were so many sick patients and not enough staff to see them.

I went back to check on the boy when a seventeen-year-old girl was wheeled into resus from minor injuries. She was deathly pale and her forehead was covered in sweat. I raced over to her.

'What's wrong?'

'My tummy hurts.'

I gently examined her. Her abdomen was rigid and she was burning up. Her blood pressure was in her boots and her pulse was racing.

'Any chance you could be pregnant?'

'I don't think so.'

The nurse had just finished taking bloods. 'What next?'

'Run a bag of Hartmanns through and catheterise her. Do a pregnancy test on the urine dip.'

It was positive. I didn't think she had an ectopic pregnancy, but she needed to go to theatre now. I grabbed the anaesthetist to take over while I called the gynaecology registrar. He wanted me to send her straight to theatre but it wasn't quite that simple. The gynae department was in another building and I had to call an ambulance to move her. It took forever to answer all the operator's questions. The closest wagon was ten minutes away.

She'd needed four litres of fluid to keep her blood pressure up and was now struggling to breathe. The anaesthetist went with her in the ambulance while I went back to the minivan passengers. Two hours later we heard that she'd died on the table. She'd had a silent miscarriage that had become infected. I couldn't believe it. I'd never lost someone that young before. Everyone in the department was shaken, but there were still patients waiting to be seen and there was no time to process what had happened. At the end of the shift I went around thanking everyone for their efforts overnight. The senior sister told me that the gynae theatre team were getting three days of compassionate leave as well as counselling to help them cope. The A&E staff simply carried on as before. It was all part of the job.

Halfway through my PhD I had an abstract accepted for a surgical conference along with another registrar doing research. We'd paid to attend the conference dinner and got chatting to the consultant seated between us. He managed to cajole the whole table into going on to a nightclub. We all piled into the taxi, which pulled up outside a lap-dancing club. The doorman obviously knew the consultant and we were ushered in without having to queue. As soon as we were inside, he went behind a red curtained area to be entertained in private. The rest of us sat down on a sofa. One of the girls working there asked me if I wanted a dance. I shook my head. I was trying to work out how long I would have to wait before I could make my excuses and leave. The only other woman in the group was an anaesthetic consultant and I could tell she was equally shocked. She leaned towards me and said that she'd get us a cab home after she'd been to the loo. As she got up to go, another consultant sat next to me, patted my knee and told me how much he loved this place. 'It doesn't count as cheating,' he said, 'because the dancers aren't real women.'

I turned thirty towards the end of my PhD and had a mid-life crisis. When I was a medical student I'd planned to be Wales's first female trauma surgeon, married with three children by the age of twenty-nine. Instead, I hadn't seen the inside of an operating room for three years and I was still single. I'd had a few relationships here and there but none of them had lasted more than a couple of months.

I was desperately lonely. I needed someone to look after now the patients had gone. Instead of feeling sorry for myself, I signed up to run the London Marathon and got two cats from the local rescue centre. I chose an eleven-year-old black cat with a cloudy eye called Picket, who never stopped purring. He'd been there for thirteen months because no one wanted a half-blind cat. On my way out of the shelter I saw a fat tabby called Charlie who'd lost most of his hair through stress and I had to take him as well. They could keep each other company while I was out at work. I had now become the cliché I used to joke about – the single crazy cat lady – but I didn't care. The cats gave me a reason to get up in the morning and a reason to go home. They loved me, and they let me love them, and that was enough.

With a couple of months left of my PhD I'd got almost all the results I needed. I still had a huge stack of scientific papers to review and appraise before I could start writing my thesis but I had other priorities. I needed to get a registrar job. I was shortlisted for the rotation in East Anglia and it took five hours to drive to Cambridge for the interview at the Deanery, the regional organisation responsible for postgraduate medical training. I was too tired to be nervous and, despite a fierce grilling, I got the job. The first two years would be split between Cambridge and Bury St Edmunds. I broke into tears in the car park outside the Deanery. The four years I'd just sacrificed had been worth it. Now all I had to do was find a house to rent on the other side of the country, finish my work in the lab and remember how to operate.

Chapter 12

After fourteen years, the day had finally arrived for me to leave Cardiff and move to Bury St Edmunds. Instead of being ten minutes away from Daljit and Bethan, there would now be hundreds of miles between us. Tears fell down my face as I locked my house for the last time. I was going from a place I knew like the back of my hand to a city where I knew nothing and no one. Where were the supermarkets? The vets? The cheapest petrol stations? How did I get to the hospital? The things I had taken for granted were gone.

I'd given myself two days to get settled in before I started as a breast surgery registrar at Addenbrooke's Hospital in Cambridge. My first job was to work out what to wear. After spending four years in jeans I had no idea what would give me that 'no longer a junior but not quite the boss' vibe. I didn't have much money to spare after paying for a removal company, rental bonds and deposits. A quick trip to the local shopping centre for some separates that didn't need ironing would have to do.

I spent the evenings sitting on my sofa flicking through surgical textbooks. I hadn't realised it would take three weeks to get broadband and Sky connected, so there was literally nothing else to do. I told myself that I'd be fine, but deep down I was scared. I was certain that I'd forgotten how to operate. I couldn't remember the basics, like whether the blue button on the diathermy pen was used for cutting or coagulating. It's the equivalent of getting into a car and forgetting which pedal to use for braking. The anatomy I once knew like the back of my hand was a distant memory. The only saving grace was that I'd done breast surgery as a house officer. I hoped it would all come rushing back to me.

The breast unit was tucked away down one of the side corridors, out of sight and mind from the rest of the surgical department. My first day started with a clinic. I walked into the room but it was empty. One of the nurses saw me inside and stuck her head around the door.

'We don't start until nine. Go and get yourself a cup of coffee.'

I brought a cup of tea back and sat waiting for people to arrive. A woman burst in carrying a list of patients. 'I'm Diane, the nurse specialist. You'll be shadowing me today. Have you done breast surgery before?'

'Only as a house officer and that was years ago.'

'Right. Come with me.'

I followed her into the clinic room. I was a little put-out that one of the consultants wasn't showing me what to do, but I got the feeling that you didn't say no to Diane. When she was satisfied I could examine a lump and knew what to do when I'd found one, I was given patients of my own.

The first woman I saw didn't have a lump. She had a painful left breast. Just like the next five women I saw. I'd heard Diane explain that the pain was actually coming from the muscles of the chest wall, not the breast, and soon had a reassuring patter down to a tee. I was amazed at how many women weren't wearing the right-size bra. Either their bra straps were too long, the elastic had gone in the back or the cups were too small, meaning breast tissue bulged out the sides. I'd never appreciated how heavy breasts can be and was shocked when Diane said that a pair of 36Cs weighed over a kilogram.

The clinics could be monotonous, but I enjoyed being able to reassure most of the women I saw that they didn't have cancer. After a couple of weeks, I did find something suspicious and it was hard not to let out a little squeak. The lady was in her sixties and had noticed the lump a few weeks earlier. I mentally ran through a checklist in my head while I continued to examine her. The breast was now divided into quadrants – upper, lower, inner and outer. Each quadrant was further divided into three segments according to the numbers on a clock face. Hers was in the left upper outer quadrant at two o'clock, five centimetres from the nipple. It was about two centimetres in diameter and felt hard and irregular to touch. I was fairly certain it was a cancer.

While she was getting dressed, I said, 'I'm going to send you for a mammogram. Would you mind if I came with you?'

Patients had previously asked me if it hurt and I had no idea. I'd never had one.

The radiographer was warm and friendly. She asked the patient to stand close to the machine before lifting her breast on to the X-ray plate. Another plate was lowered down on top, squashing it flat.

'Deep breath. This might pinch a bit.'

The radiographer then moved the woman's breast so it could be squashed from side to side for the second image.

'Same again. Deep breath.'

'Did that hurt?' I asked.

'Not really.'

I left her in the waiting room while I went to look at her mammograms with the radiologist. I couldn't get my head around them at first.

'It's like a 3D grid,' the radiologist said. 'The first film shows me where the cancer lies on a line from the sternum to the armpit. The lateral film tells me how far above or below the nipple the cancer is.'

It started to make sense. She then did an ultrasound. As I looked at the screen I could see an obvious cancer with an irregular outline and a dark fuzzy centre.

'We're going to need to do a biopsy.'

The nurse passed the radiologist some local anaesthetic to numb the skin before pushing the biopsy gun into the lump. It made a loud bang when she fired it. I gave the woman an appointment to come back next week for the results and suggested she brought someone with to her to pass the time while she sat in the waiting room.

After a couple of weeks I was able to observe women being told they had cancer. The first patient was in her fifties and she'd come with her husband. It had been picked up through screening and because she hadn't felt a lump, she wasn't expecting the news. I watched them collapse as the diagnosis sank in. Paula, her breast-care nurse, handed her a tissue. The consultant gave them a moment or two and then carried on.

'It's a small cancer and it's good that we've caught it early. You're going to need an operation to treat it called a lumpectomy and I'll also remove some of the lymph nodes under your arm to make sure that it hasn't spread. The surgery is straightforward but there are some complications. Some ladies get permanent swelling of their arm called lymphoedema. There's also the risk of scarring and asymmetry afterwards. The blue dye we use to find the lymph nodes can stain a small patch of skin blue for up to a year. After the surgery you'll need a course of radiotherapy to the breast and we'll start you on a tablet called tamoxifen for five years to stop it coming back.'

I was struggling to take in all that information and I wasn't the one who'd been told they had cancer. There was so much to cover. As soon it was over, I rushed to my bag for a notebook to write everything down. Paula handed me a pile of leaflets.

'It's all in here.'

They were given to every cancer patient and covered everything from surgical consent to chemotherapy. Now I had crib sheets I could take home and memorise.

A couple of weeks later, one of the consultants asked me if I wanted to break bad news myself. The patient was seventy-two with a small cancer that needed a simple lumpectomy. I thought I was ready. I double-checked her notes, asked Paula to go with me and knocked on the door. The lady made it easy for me. She'd been expecting the news because her sister had been diagnosed three years earlier and knew all about the surgery. I kept stumbling and forgot crucial pieces of information. Paula had to keep interrupting me to fill in the gaps. I was trying to repeat what I'd heard the consultants say but their words didn't feel right coming from my mouth. I was glad when it was over.

'How was that?' asked Paula.

'It was awful. I made such a hash of it.'

'Don't be silly. It was your first time. I've seen far worse from some of our other registrars. You just need to practise. Figure out what phrases work for you. You're good at this. You'll get there.'

One morning one of the consultants came out of an examination room with tears in his eyes. I didn't know what was going on. I'd missed the start of the clinic because I'd been on the ward seeing a patient. He sat down, stared at the floor and said, 'It's not fair.'

Diane took me aside and told me he'd just seen a woman in her twenties who'd presented with a cancer last week but her CT scan had shown deposits in her liver and lungs. It took a moment to sink in. She was younger than me. She couldn't be cured with an operation. Her chance of still being alive this time next year was slim. The enormity of my job started to take hold. Breast cancer didn't just affect women in their sixties and seventies. I watched my boss take a deep breath.

'Right. Who's next?'

I realised I wasn't the only one who put on a mask at work.

I was nervous about being back in an operating theatre. My anatomy was rusty and I didn't want to look incompetent. The repetition of scrubbing up helped me relax so I could start to concentrate on what lay ahead. The first case was a lady in her sixties. Her breasts were huge and must have weighed more than a kilogram each. She had a palpable lump of DCIS, a non-invasive form of breast cancer. Left alone, it would almost certainly become invasive with the potential to spread to her lymph nodes and beyond.

Although I knew where the cancer was from the mammograms, it was impossible to find now she was lying flat on the operating table. Instead of her breasts being compressed between the plates, they flopped flat across her chest, spilling on to the table below. I longed to be back in the abdomen, where everything was where it was meant to be. My boss came through to join me.

After prepping and draping her chest, he pushed her breast up into its natural position and put a cross on the skin above the cancer. Then he let the breast fall away, picked up the scalpel and cut into the skin before switching to diathermy. He made his way through the breast until he came close to the lump.

'Have a feel.'

'It's harder than the rest of the tissue.'

He passed me the diathermy pen.

'Keep your fingers over it and cut all the way around, down to the chest wall.'

The heat of the diathermy melted through the breast as I worked. Keeping my fingers over it meant a rim of normal tissue was removed with the cancer. It was the margin of safety needed to make sure that all the cells were excised. Everything was done by touch, not anatomy. As I cut through the final strands of tissue connecting the cancer to the fascia beneath, my consultant told me to stop.

'Put in the marking sutures while it's still in position.'

I'd forgotten about that part. Every cancer was marked with two sutures to help the pathologist orientate it. The front of the tumour, closest to the skin, had a stitch with short ends, and the top of the tumour, nearest the head, had long ends. The only way I could remember it was to keep repeating 'SALSA' in my head – Short Anterior, Long Superior.

The next case was a woman who'd come through breast screening. She had a small, low-grade cancer but there was nothing to feel. Earlier that morning, the radiologists had inserted a guide wire into the centre of it and new mammograms gave us a target to aim for. Because her cancer was invasive, there was a chance that it had spread to the lymph nodes in her armpit. We were going to remove the first one, the sentinel node. If it was clear, the other nodes would be as well. My consultant used two techniques to find the node. Before she came to theatre, a radioisotope had been injected near the woman's nipple that would get taken up by the node. In theatre, a blue dye was injected under the nipple skin that flowed through tiny lymph vessels to the armpit. The goal was to find a hot blue node.

My boss had said that I could do this part of the operation. I held the gamma probe over the nipple and heard a loud screeching sound. As I moved it towards the armpit, the sound fell away to silence before getting louder again. I'd found the node. The scrub nurse passed me a small syringe full of bright-blue dye, which I injected just

under the areola. As I massaged the breast for five minutes I could see faint blue lines spreading out under the
skin. I made an incision below the hairline of the armpit
and carefully retracted the fat until I saw a thin streak of
blue. It had worked! I followed the blue lymph vessel
deeper into the fat until I came across a juicy blue node.
I turned to my boss, beaming under the mask.

'Now check it with the probe.'

As I did, the probe started screeching. This was definitely the one. I took the node out and passed it to the
scrub nurse. My first solo operation. The consultant then
took over to show me how to remove the breast cancer. I
was sure he would make a cut right over the wire. Instead
he put a cross on the opposite side of the breast. I'd
assumed that the entry point of the wire was directly
over the cancer. He said, 'Sometimes the radiographers
push the wire in from the other side because it's an
easier angle.'

He then started tapping the breast, making the wire
bounce.

'The more it moves, the closer you are to the cancer.'

He cut down over that spot and kept going until he
found the wire, following it through the breast until he
reached the cancer. He let me have a feel inside and I
could just about tell the difference between the cancer
and the breast, but if the wire hadn't been there I wouldn't
have had a clue. He fished the cancer out, marked it and
closed up the wounds.

I grew to love the breast lists and was gradually allowed
to do most of the operating. Any woman who needed a
mastectomy had a drain put under the skin to remove

tissue fluid that collected under the skin flaps. They would stay in hospital until there was no more fluid, which could take up to a week, and I got to know my patients quite well. I remember one particular lady in her eighties with a large attentive family. The nurses on the ward had warned me to try to avoid them because they could talk and talk and talk. She was the last patient I had to see after spending all day in theatre. My heart sank when I saw all her family around her bed. After checking her wound and agreeing that she could go home tomorrow, her daughter asked me, 'Does breast cancer run in families?'

'It can do.'

'So is that why one of my nephews has testicular cancer? And why doesn't my other son have it? And could we all get cancer? Is it catching? Will their children get it too?'

I looked up to see her two nephews waiting to hear my reply. I gently sat down next to my patient on her bed and spent the next hour carefully explaining cancer and genetics until everyone understood. By the time I'd finished, it had gone eight o'clock. I could see that the daughter was going to ask another question, but I had to cut her off. I was flagging and it would take me an hour to get home.

'I'm really sorry, but I've got to check on another patient.'

'Of course. Sorry, doctor. Thank you for your time.'

I made my escape, swearing under my breath about how long that had taken. On Monday as I walked past the nurses' office on the way to clinic, Paula called out to me.

'There's a present for you.'

'Really?'

'Yes, from the Italian lady with the large family.'

She handed me the gift. It was a Barbie doll wearing a large, white, hand-crocheted dress hiding a toilet roll underneath. My gran used to have one that took pride of place in her bathroom.

'Wow. I don't know what to say.'

'She wanted to say thank you for taking the time to talk to her family.'

I was humbled. It was the first gift I'd ever had from a patient and it wasn't for my surgical prowess or diagnostic skills. It was simply for taking the time to listen.

Although I liked being back in theatres, I was dreadfully lonely, and as much as I loved my cats, they weren't great company. I had no local friends. The registrars were married with lives of their own, and all the junior doctors lived in Cambridge. When I did make the effort to meet them in a club, I felt awkward. I was desperate to have a couple of drinks and let my hair down on the dancefloor but I couldn't be part of the gang at night knowing I might have to bollock someone the following day. Instead, I threw myself into writing up my thesis. For three nights each week I fell into a sad routine: get up at a quarter to five, leave the house at half-six, get home at seven, sleep for three hours, get up at ten, order a large pizza and a two-litre bottle of Pepsi Max, write until one then go back to bed.

Every month there were mandatory training days, and the first was in West Suffolk Hospital in Bury St Edmunds, where I would be working next. The day started with a colorectal surgeon telling us how to run a successful private practice, followed by Mr O'Riordan, an upper gastrointestinal surgeon. He told us about a recent visit to a hospital in the United States. I was captivated by his talk as he described what was possible when clinicians and managers worked together using data to improve patient care. He stood out from the other surgeons in his sharp suit and stripy tie. He had interesting thoughts and ideas, and I hoped I'd be able to work for him the following year.

While I grew to love the rhythm of breast surgery, I hated the on-calls. The registrars were usually in their final year of training and they could handle most things by themselves. I was the first year-one registrar to work there and must have been one hell of a shock for the consultants. Although breast surgery was the perfect speciality to help me find my feet again, it was the worst possible job to help me handle the acute take. I never saw the general surgeons during the day because the breast team used separate theatres, so they had no idea who I was or what I could do. And they soon realised that I couldn't do anything. Because I wasn't operating on the abdomen anymore, I'd become deskilled and couldn't even do an appendicectomy by myself. What had I done to deserve this?

The shifts were twelve hours long. Three days on, one day off, three nights on, two days off, before going back to normal working hours. Add in the one-hour commute and I was doing fourteen-hour days. I was looking after patients who'd had complex liver and pancreatic surgery with no idea how to manage them. There were three different ITUs to cover and a busy A&E as well as the wards.

When I arrived in the handover room for my first day shift, I was told there were two laparoscopic appendicectomies that needed doing. I'd never even heard of a laparoscopic appendicectomy. During my PhD, surgery had been transformed and many operations were now done as keyhole procedures using cameras and ports. Faced with a roomful of strangers, I desperately asked if anyone could show me how to do it. Thankfully, the night registrar agreed to stay on. I tried to grasp the basics of what he was doing, mentally taking notes for the next time. The second case was booked for the afternoon and I had to find another registrar to help me. There was no way I was letting the consultant find out that I didn't know how to do one.

The night shifts were worse. The hospital never stopped. I barely saw the inside of the mess to grab a cup of tea, let alone a quick nap on the sofa. I was always reviewing patients or operating. Well, actually, I wasn't operating. I was watching pissed-off consultants operating in the middle of the night because I couldn't do a bowel resection by myself. I could see them deflate every morning at handover when they saw it was me they were on with. Three months in and I still hadn't mastered the laparoscopic appendicectomy. There were several ways to do it and everyone who helped me used a different method. One night, yet again, I'd had to call one of the consultants to come and help. I hadn't spent much time with him before and wasn't sure how he'd react. I prepared myself for the worst. By the time the patient was asleep it had just gone midnight. While we were scrubbing, he said, 'Right. I'm going to make you do this from skin to skin. I'm going to teach you one safe way so you can do it by yourself.'

He took the next ninety minutes to walk me through,

explaining the reasoning behind each step, getting me to repeat things so I'd remember what to do. I hated every minute of it. I could see the theatre staff looking at the clock. I just wanted him to take over and end the torture. But he didn't. He knew I had to go through this. By the time we were finished my scrubs were plastered to me from the sweat that had run down my back and legs and there was a damp patch on the gown when I ripped it off.

'Thank you,' I said.

'No problem. We've all been in your shoes. It's just that some of us don't remember it.'

The worst part of each night shift was at the end, when the handover had finished. The adrenaline that had kept me going for the last twelve hours was about to run out and I still had to drive home. There were days when I couldn't remember if I'd skipped a red light. To help me stay awake I started downing a can of Red Bull when there were only five patients left, hoping it would kick in by the time I reached the car. The exhausted part of my brain reasoned that if I drove faster, I would get home quicker. With the windows fully open and a whole pack of chewing gum in my mouth, I convinced myself I was safe to drive.

I was glad when the six months were over. I was proud that I'd coped and thought if I could handle the on-call at Addenbrooke's, I could handle anything. But it was time to move on to Bury St Edmunds and hopefully a quieter pace of life.

Chapter 13

Right from day one, I knew I was going to love working at West Suffolk. Everyone was so friendly. Unlike Addenbrooke's, where everyone stared at the ground as they rushed past, porters and nurses now stopped to say hello in the corridors. It was a much smaller hospital and I knew the canteen was good. I could still remember the warm scones from the training day. I was going to be there for eighteen months splitting my time between three specialities, starting with colorectal surgery.

I was back in my comfort zone now I was operating in the abdomen again. I learned how to mobilise the bowel by freeing the attachments to the abdominal wall and how to join the ends back together with an anastamosis. There were four colorectal nurses who helped look after the cancer patients and they taught me where to site a stoma so it wouldn't get in the way of a skirt waistband or a golf swing. Two of them, Maggie and Nicky, quickly became good friends.

In the third week of the job, a man with a low rectal cancer was coming in for an abdomino-perineal resection. It had been years since I'd seen one as an SHO and I'd forgotten just how big a procedure it was. When a rectal tumour is almost at the anal verge, the anus is removed with the rectum. The remaining end of the colon is brought through a hole in the abdominal skin leaving the patient with a permanent colostomy. My SHO had to hold the retractor while I got to watch my boss working between the legs as he cut around the anal canal. I reached deep inside the pelvis to push down on the strands of tissue separating my fingers from the outside world as he worked up to meet me. Once the bowel was free, I pulled it up and out of the way. I looked inside again to see my consultant's face staring at me between the patient's legs.

I was seriously considering specialising in colorectal surgery. The only thing stopping me was the anterior resection, an operation for higher rectal cancers mostly done down a deep, dark hole. No one ever looked like they were enjoying it. Male patients were always harder because of their narrow pelvis.

One morning after a particularly difficult case, I'd just fired the linear stapler to detach the cancer from the rectum and all that was left was to join up the ends. Instead of hand-sewing the anastomosis in the depths, I would be using a staple gun. The consultant placed a purse-string suture around the open end of the colon and tied it around the head of an anvil. It was like a metal mushroom with a sharp end on the stalk. It was my job to insert the gun into the anus until it was flush against the rectal staple line. My boss pushed the stalk of the anvil through the rectum into the head of the gun and told me to fire it. I squeezed the trigger and heard a satisfying clunk before gently removing the gun.

'Fuck.'

'What's wrong?' I asked. I couldn't see from where I was standing.

'It's not worked. The gun can't have fired properly.'

It was meant to insert two circular lines of staples while removing a doughnut of tissue in the middle, creating a water-tight anastomosis. I opened the gun to see two doughnuts but the staples were still there. The rectal stump was even smaller than before and there wasn't enough room to close it with the linear stapler. The only option was to join the bowel by hand. My boss looked at the scrub nurse. 'Someone get Liz a pillow to kneel on.'

I spent the next hour on my knees pushing my fist into the patient's perineum so my boss could reach the tiny stump deep inside. My arm was killing me by the time he'd finished. The theatre sister took pity on me and bleeped the on-call registrar to come and close while I went to stretch and find some ibuprofen.

The on-calls were much quieter, and because I lived close to the hospital, I could go home to sleep at night once everything was sorted. It was such a luxury to be in my own bed instead of a stale on-call room. All the other registrars were in their first or second year of training and I no longer felt embarrassed about my lack of experience. I was now confident enough to do an easy laparascopic appendicectomy by myself and the consultants didn't mind coming in for the more difficult cases.

One night there were two appendicectomies to do. Both patients were young and fit, and I was looking forward to some nice, easy surgery to boost my logbook. I'd been gossiping with one of the nurses on the ward for ages when I realised theatres still hadn't rung to say they were sending for the first case. It was almost nine o'clock. I rang them to find out what was taking so long.

'We finished them both an hour ago. The consultant came in to do them.'

The on-call consultant loved operating so much that he'd come in to operate without me knowing. I'd not experienced that particular style of training before.

Meanwhile, I had to learn how to train someone myself. Sarah, one of the other registrars, told me about the SHO she had to train in her last job. He was desperate to operate and not remotely interested in the patients on the wards. All he wanted to do was cut. He could talk the talk and sounded like he knew what he was doing but his skills weren't up to scratch and she said she was often left to pick up the pieces.

One day when they didn't have much to do, he'd managed to persuade one of the colorectal consultants to let him do a flexible sigmoidoscopy to look inside the lower part of the large bowel. Sarah got a frantic call from one of the nurses.

'Can you come to endoscopy?'

'What's wrong?'

'That's right. Room two.'

When she arrived, the SHO said, 'I think I've found a tumour.'

Sarah took one look at the screen and had to stop herself swearing out loud. She was looking at a cervix. He'd put the endoscope in the vagina instead of the anus. The patient hadn't said anything and the nurse didn't realise until it was too late.

One Sunday morning I was bleeped to A&E to see a man who'd been stabbed with a pair of scissors. I rushed down expecting to see blood everywhere, but he was sitting up on a trolley. He was rather overweight. When I examined him, I could see a small hole about two inches above his belly button. I put on a pair of gloves and gently probed through the fat. I couldn't get deep enough to feel if the scissors had pierced the rectus sheath below. I'd need to explore the wound in theatre. I bleeped the on-call consultant, who told me to crack on while he finished the ward round. I rang theatres and spoke to the nurse in charge.

'I've got a wound I need to explore under local. It shouldn't take long.'

'There's a trauma case going on at the moment so the anaesthetist is busy.'

'That's all right. I'm not expecting it to be anything. I just need a minor tray. I can manage without a scrub nurse.'

'I'm not really meant to do this,' she said, 'but OK. Bring him up to theatre five.'

I prepped and draped his tummy before injecting local anaesthetic. I used a retractor to pull the fat away so I could explore the wound. My heart sank. There was a hole in the sheath that I could push my little finger through. Shit. Now he'd need a laparotomy to open up his abdomen and see how bad the damage was. And I had an awake patient lying on a narrow operating table who could be bleeding inside. 'We're going to need to operate.

The hole's a bit bigger than I thought. Are you OK to stay here on the table while I sort things out?'

'Yes, but could you get me a blanket? It's a bit cold.'

I pulled off my gown and went into the theatre next door to talk to Jenny, the on-call anaesthetist.

'What's up?'

'That wound I was exploring under local next door? Well, there's a hole in the rectus sheath and he's going to need a laparotomy.'

'Seriously? I knew this wasn't a good idea. I'm going to be tied up here for an hour and the registrar's busy on the maternity suite. Is he safe to stay there?'

'I think so.' After putting in a line and finding a nurse to repeat his obs, I perched on a stool next to him. My boss turned up and he wasn't happy.

'I thought you said it was a shallow wound?'

'I thought it was.'

'How much longer do we have to wait?'

At that moment Jenny came in and we went to get scrubbed. I cut open his abdomen to find a litre of clotted blood inside. Jenny gasped. 'Has he really spent the last hour lying on an operating table with all of that inside him?'

The scissors had pierced one of the large blood vessels in the mesentery, an apron of fat that carries blood vessels to the bowel, narrowly missing the aorta. He was lucky to survive, and I was lucky he hadn't arrested when I was watching over him.

After six months of colorectal surgery, it was time to move on to breast surgery. In between the mastectomies and lumpectomies, the theatre lists were scattered with gallbladders and inguinal hernia repairs. I was now a year-two registrar and felt like I'd developed superpowers overnight. The day before, I didn't have the confidence to start a laparoscopic gallbladder without a consultant next to me. Now I was happy to crack on while my new boss sat in the coffee room, giving me time to get in and have a look around before coming to oversee. Simply moving up a grade had given me a huge boost, even though my surgical ability hadn't changed.

It felt good to be back doing breast surgery again. I was more comfortable in clinic when it came to breaking bad news. Gone were the back-breaking three-hour colorectal operations. They were replaced with quick, clean breast surgeries and lots of lovely hand-sewing. My consultant let me start every operation, but the moment I got stuck, he'd come and take over. I began to notice that whenever I asked a theatre nurse to call him, he would wait another ten to fifteen minutes before coming through, giving me time to see if I could work it out myself.

It was actually a great way of learning how to cope, especially when I was operating at night. Whenever I was out of my depth, I would spend ages panicking over whether to call my boss or not. The longer I faffed, the later it got and the harder it was to make a decision. When I did finally call, the anxiety lifted and I could concentrate again. I'd often worked out what to do by the time they arrived. One night, the consultant let me in on a secret. 'There are only two reasons that you get stuck. You can't see what you're doing or the hole is too small. Move the retractors and make the hole bigger. Skin heals from side to side, not end to end.'

The breast theatre staff were a tightly knit unit and it was great to be part of their team. One morning we had a locum Russian anaesthetist. He was trying to understand why my consultant didn't call himself doctor.

'It's because surgeons were originally barbers,' said my boss.

'And you are Miss?'

'Yes,' I said.

'It's very confusing. In my country, we keep it simple. We have Surgeon, and Surgeon Lady.'

I loved that. Surgeon Lady it was.

I found out that my next post would be in Norwich, another busy teaching hospital. I was going to miss Bury St Edmunds. It also meant I had to look for another place to rent. The hour-long commute was not an option after the twelve-hour shifts I'd be working. I submitted my PhD thesis and spent another month cramming for the viva. I passed this oral exam with some minor corrections and was now a double doctor. Or Dr Miss Dr Surgeon Lady, to be exact. Sadly, the homework didn't stop. Every year, registrars were expected to complete audits, present research at conferences and get papers published in scientific journals. When I wasn't working or sleeping I would often go out with the juniors on Thursdays to Brazilia, a nightclub that was as cheesy as it sounded. It was fun at first to let my hair down but the hangovers got harder to handle in theatre the next day. I'd coped as an SHO because I was only holding a retractor, but now I was expected to do most of the operating myself, I needed a clear head.

For my final six months at West Suffolk, I was going

to be doing upper gastrointestinal surgery with Mr O'Riordan. I'd heard from the other registrars that he was one of the best trainers in the Deanery. He was also the nicest surgeon to be on-call with and always rang to see what was going on before he went to sleep. I had a new SHO, Annie, and we instantly hit it off.

Part of the job involved learning how to do gastroscopies. I watched Mr O'Riordan do a couple and then it was my turn. He looked at me and said, 'Open your mouth,' before spraying local anaesthetic down the back of my throat. It was disgusting. It tasted of bananas, which I hate. He was grinning. 'You need to know what it tastes like so you can tell the patients what to expect.'

The nurse brought the next lady in. After spraying her throat, I asked her to bite down on a tongue guard. The gastroscope had two wheels on either side that moved the end up or down, left or right. I pushed it into her mouth while staring at the monitor. Using my thumb, I guided it into her oesophagus. Once I reached the stomach I used both hands to turn the wheels to have a good look around. Mr O'Riordan started laughing. 'Stand up straight.'

I stopped for a moment and realised I was leaning way over to the right with my ear almost on my shoulder as I tried to see round the corner.

'You have to move the scope, not your body.'

'This is harder than it looks.'

Mr O'Riordan had a very different training style. He expected me to start every case and do most of the operating with Annie assisting me. Most of his patients had laparoscopic surgery to remove gallbladders or fix hernias. He'd sit on a stool in the corner until I had the camera and ports in place and then he'd wander off to have a coffee or chat to someone in another theatre. He must have had a sixth sense because he would always magically reappear just as I was about to ask the nurse to find him. Instead of scrubbing up to help, he'd simply tell me what to do. He never got flustered or angry or impatient. Because he was so calm, I stayed calm and nearly always finished each operation. We both knew how important it was for me to be able to work things out myself because one day he wouldn't be around.

One weekend, I got bleeped to A&E to see a man with surgical emphysema. It normally happens after chest trauma when a rib cracks and pierces the lung. Air escapes into the soft tissues of the chest and tracks up into the neck. The neck swells and it feels and sounds like a rustling crisp packet.

'How did he do it?'

'You're not going to believe this.'

'Try me.'

'Well, twice a day for the last couple of years he's been going to his garage and blowing compressed air up his arse. He must have perforated something.'

'Seriously?' I picked up the patient's notes and went to talk to him. His voice was hoarse and he felt short of breath. Amazingly, he had no abdominal pain. I looked at his X-rays. There was free air in his abdomen that must have tracked up to his neck. He was going to need an operation to repair the hole in his rectum. I started to explain that he needed to have a laparotomy and might need a temporary colostomy, depending on how things looked inside. He grasped my wrist and looked up at me.

'What am I going to tell my wife?'

I didn't know what to say.

I had two months left at West Suffolk and had just finished one of the busiest on-call weekends I'd ever had. For forty-eight hours I literally hadn't stopped. I turned up to the Monday-morning ward round still in scrubs from the night before. The piece of surgical tape I'd used to stop my scrub top flashing my bra to the world when I bent over was long gone. There were bags on the bags under my eyes, and as I looked down at the floor to mentally prepare myself for the handover I noticed that I'd forgotten to clean the blood splatters from my white theatre shoes.

As we snaked our way around the ward seeing patients, I realised just how many mistakes I'd made due to the lack of sleep. I'd forgotten to check some of the scan results and a couple of the patients were a lot sicker than I'd first thought. The consultant became more and more frustrated. 'Why didn't you get a scan? Where's the blood gas? What's the amylase? Why haven't you booked them for theatre?' It went on and on. As uncomfortable as it was, I knew he was right. Patients' lives were at stake. By the time the ward round finished, my voice was nothing more than a mumbled whisper. I'd had enough. I ended up walking on autopilot to the colorectal nurses' office. Thankfully, Jean and Carol were in. I slid to a crumpled heap on the floor and sobbed, 'I'm done. I can't take it anymore.'

Carol put the kettle on while Jean helped me up to a chair and gave me a hug. She locked the door and asked me what had happened. I filled her in. 'I can't take it anymore. I'm exhausted. How is anyone meant to function without sleep? I thought surgery would be enough to make up for the non-existent social life and being hundreds of miles from my friends but now I'm not so sure. The way I feel right now, I'd rather stack shelves than be a surgeon.'

'I'm going to let you in on a secret,' said Jean. 'Every single registrar has felt like this at one time or another. Every single one. And look at them now, all successful consultants. Some days are worse than others. We all know you're good at your job. It was just a weekend from hell, that's all.'

My eyelids were starting to droop. I'd been running on empty for the last couple of hours and needed to crash. I gave them a hug and dragged myself home.

Over the next few days, I plastered on a fake smile and carried on. I was back to being happy, helpful Liz. I could feel myself starting to get depressed again. I wasn't sleeping well and would spend hours staring into space, only getting off the sofa to feed the cats or go to the loo. I still wasn't sure if I was cut out to be a surgeon but the thought of studying to do something else was daunting. I needed money to pay the mortgage and couldn't face going back to university. I found a medical careers coach online. She gave me a workbook to fill in that only made me more depressed. My life was incredibly unbalanced. I had sacrificed almost everything – friends, hobbies, fun – to become a surgeon. She suggested that I look into management consultancy or the pharma industry but neither of them excited me. All I could do was keep going through the motions at work until I came up with an escape plan.

Summer arrived and my mood changed with it. Ironically I became more confident at work as I knew that surgery would soon be a thing of the past. I decided to start flattering the consultants in the hope that it would stop some of them being quite so picky. I started with Mr O'Riordan. He was always nice so I thought he would be good to practise on. He wore Paul Smith suits with not-quite-matching stripy socks and ties. I began by asking him to show me his socks. One of the other consultants was passing and he joined in, proudly displaying his grey socks from a supermarket that cost a lot less. It became a morning ritual. One of the consultants was in a band and whenever we were on-call together I would ask him how rehearsals were going. I talked to another about his children, and let another moan to me about his wife. It was like magic. Feminine charm and gentle manipulation meant I had them eating out of the palm of my hand. It calmed them down in theatre and it was fun too. I had finally found a way to be me in this male-dominated world without damaging my reputation. I knew where my lines were and how far I was comfortable to push them. I actually enjoyed going to work again.

Annie had a pair of gold ballet flats that she often wore to work. Over the next week several of the female house officers turned up in the same shoes. I was envious because I couldn't find any to fit my size-nine feet. The song 'Black and Gold' by Sam Sparro was always on the radio and it gave me an idea. One weekend on-call, I sent out an email to the entire surgical department asking everyone to wear something black or gold on Friday. I didn't think anyone would do it, but when Friday came around, all the juniors were wearing something in those colours, as well as Mr O'Riordan and two more consultants. After that, each week a junior doctor took it in turns to choose a colour. Friday was now my favourite day of the week. I wondered what the nurses thought when we all turned up wearing pink shirts and tops for the ward round. It was such a simple idea but it had a huge impact and brought everyone closer together as a team.

With one month left, I went to Paris for a long weekend with Bethan. She travelled down from Cardiff and we treated ourselves to a bottle of bubbly in the champagne bar before getting on the Eurostar. Two glasses later on an empty stomach, I ended up telling her that I had a crush on Mr O'Riordan. I couldn't believe I'd said it out loud.

'Seriously?'

'Yes. No. Oh, I don't know. Nothing's going to happen. Besides, he's got baggage. He's ten years older than me and he's been married before. It's just harmless flirting in theatre. Besides, I'm going to Norwich in two weeks.'

Nothing more was said.

A couple of weeks later, Mr O'Riordan had a barbecue for the surgical team. I'd never been to a consultant's house before. He lived in an old listed building full of wooden beams with a large garden out the back. After dropping off the brownies I'd made, I went over to see what all the juniors were looking at and immediately fell in love. In a fenced-off section of the garden was Chester, his chocolate Labrador. He was adorable.

My last day arrived and I spent a lot of it crying. I was so sad to leave. Annie had made gingerbread lady surgeons and one of the secretaries had bought me flowers. Mr O'Riordan came into the doctor's office to wish me well. He'd baked a cake and was carrying a huge box. Inside it was a pair of black and gold wellies and some Paul Smith stripy socks. Annie couldn't stop grinning. 'I've been trying to get him to buy you some gold Christian Louboutins so you wouldn't feel left out, but these are perfect!'

Maybe he liked me too. But it was too late. I was about to move to Norwich and I still needed to work out what I might do if I quit surgery.

Chapter 14

After an exhausting day unpacking boxes, it was nine o'clock and I was ready for bed. I collapsed on the sofa with a cup of tea and flicked through my emails to double-check what I was doing in the morning, when I saw one from Mr O'Riordan. It was so nice of him to wish me luck in my new job. Except he wasn't. He was asking me out.

It knocked me for six. I'd only flirted with him in theatre because I knew nothing would ever happen. It was harmless. He was my boss. I rang Bethan. 'Mr O'Riordan has just asked me out.'

'Oh. My. God.'

'What do I do?' My heart knew that I wanted to say yes, but my head was in overdrive with questions and potential problems. 'What will all his colleagues think? What will my parents think? Oh God, I'm going to be known as the registrar that slept her way up the career ladder.'

'Do you still like him?'

'Yes.'

'Then go for it. You've got nothing to lose.'

I emailed him back and dragged myself off to bed. I was too nervous to sleep. I rushed downstairs the following morning. He'd replied. After going back and forth with on-calls and other commitments, we eventually settled on Sunday lunch in a fortnight's time. The first two weeks of work passed in a blur. I couldn't concentrate on anything. I was going on a date. It had been five years since my last one. I was thirty-four-years old and seriously out of practice.

I arranged to meet him at the pub and got there ten minutes early. I was sitting in the car muttering to myself about what a mistake this was when I saw him pull into the car park.

'Mr O'Riordan?' I couldn't bring myself to call him Dermot. In my head he was still my boss. He came over to meet me with a shy smile on his face. As he leaned over to kiss my cheek, I reached out for a very formal handshake. It was just too weird.

The food was great. It was a shame the conversation didn't match it. Outside of the safe confines of theatre, in casual clothes instead of scrubs, I didn't feel a spark. The date was more like a careers interview and I didn't want to lead him on. Later that night he called me to say how much he'd enjoyed our lunch date and asked if I wanted to go out for dinner in the week. I thought we deserved a second chance and so I said yes, hoping that he would grow on me again.

I must have changed my clothes ten times before he arrived to pick me up with a bouquet in his hand. I couldn't remember the last time a man had bought me flowers. I started to relax a bit more in his company. It was such a thrill to see the twinkle in his eye and know I was the reason behind it. Maybe I did like him after all.

We held hands in the cab on the way home until the taxi dropped him off. A few minutes later, my phone pinged. It was Dermot texting to thank me for a lovely evening. I couldn't stop smiling.

My first six months in Norwich were in paediatric surgery. I'd been looking forward to working with children again and as an added bonus I wasn't rostered to be on-call for another three weeks. There were four consultants and I was one of five registrars. The unit was quiet compared to the general surgery wards and there wasn't enough work to go around. As a result, there would often be two or three registrars at every theatre list, and because I was a general surgeon, I was at the bottom of the pile when it came to operating. One of the paediatric registrars, Risha, was lovely. Our logbooks were both low on numbers and we were frustrated at the lack of training opportunities. Between us we worked out ways to split a circumcision into parts so we'd each get to cut. She would remove one layer of the foreskin and I would remove the next. I would put in two sutures and she would put in three. After a month, I stepped back to let her do most of the operating. It mattered more to her career that she got her cases up and I knew that I was never going to switch to paediatrics. The speciality had lost its spark now I wasn't working with Tom.

The on-calls were tough. I did weeks of twelve-hour shifts and it was just like being back in Addenbrooke's. The consultants were used to senior trainees who could handle the take and I was rapidly becoming deskilled on the paediatric ward. Days were spent trying to find a registrar to give me a hand in theatre, while I had to ask consultants to come in and help at night. One consultant seemed particularly annoyed with me. Whenever we were on-call together, my nerves got the better of me and I started making stupid mistakes. I dreaded the morning ward rounds. I remember one morning when I must have looked like a complete idiot. I got the patients mixed up when I presented them and forgot crucial blood results. I couldn't wait for it to finish, thankful that at least I'd be on with a different consultant that night. I got home and put the key in the lock but the door was already open. I thought I'd been burgled. As I slowly went inside I found a bunch of flowers on the hall carpet and Dermot in the kitchen cooking me breakfast. I'd forgotten that I'd given him a key. Once we'd eaten, he gave me another hug and drove back home so I could sleep before my next shift.

After six months of paediatrics, I switched to vascular surgery and was finally going to be working for a woman. The other two registrars were on-call on my first day so it was up to me to do the ward round. My new house officer, Claire, led me around the patients. Instead of the five or six children I'd been used to, there were now over forty patients to review before heading off to clinic. It was nice to get back into the flow of general surgery but after the first couple of patients I could see Claire looking more and more confused. 'What's up?' I asked.

'Why are you asking them about their bowels? You're meant to be checking the pulses in their feet.'

I was so used to asking post-op colorectal patients whether they'd farted that I'd forgotten I was now looking after vascular patients.

One of the great things about having a female boss was not having to talk about sport all the time. We were both obsessed with *Strictly Come Dancing* and every Monday we'd pore over the weekend's results. It was so good to develop a proper relationship with her and a lot of that happened in the changing room. Having that extra time to talk about the day's operations, patients on the ward or just life in general made me decide to stick with surgery for the time being. Was this what it was like for the male registrars and their bosses? I wondered how disadvantaged I might have been as a woman, missing out on those extra opportunities for training and advice.

The surgery was varied. One day I'd be sitting down watching my boss make a fistula in the forearm for dialysis. The next, I'd be bent double for three hours holding a retractor while she connected a long graft from the groin to the ankle to try to preserve the patient's foot. Despite operating on arteries and veins, I was surprised how little blood there was. The one exception was varicose vein surgery. After marking all the bulging valves, I'd make tiny stab incisions over each spot. Then I used a small metal hook to rip out each enlarged vein before tightly wrapping the legs in bandages. The floor looked like a blood bath when it was over.

One night I had to amputate a necrotic toe from an elderly diabetic man. He'd been waiting on the emergency list for three days and kept getting bumped by more urgent cases. It was finally his turn. Once he was asleep, I cut off the bandage on his foot. One of the nurses shrieked as a stream of maggots fell on to the operating room floor. I wanted to be sick. Instead, I got down on my hands and knees to pick them all up because no one else would do it.

That was the last operation of the night and I had headed off to the canteen for a drink when I was fast-bleeped to the ward opposite theatres. I found one of my vascular patients surrounded by the crash team after having a cardiac arrest. She'd come in the day before with back pain and we'd picked up a ten-centimetre abdominal aneurysm that she didn't know she had. Sadly, because of her other medical problems, she wasn't fit enough to survive an operation to repair it. The vascular nurses had spent a lot of time counselling her about what would happen when it did eventually rupture. She was meant to go home the following day but her aneurysm had other plans.

I knew that the vascular consultant on-call had left half an hour ago. I now had a patient who wasn't fit for an elective repair but because she'd arrested opposite theatres and the anaesthetist had been walking past when the bleep went off, she was still alive. There was nothing else to do but take her to theatre. I raced across the corridor to find the sister in charge, and then called the consultant. 'The lady with the ten-centimetre aneurysm just ruptured. She arrested but the crash team brought her back. I'm taking her to theatre now.'

'OK. I'll turn around and meet you there.'

Time is of the essence when dealing with a rupture. The only thing that will give the patient a fighting chance is getting a clamp on the top end of the aorta so the anaesthetists can resuscitate them. She arrested again. There wasn't time to scrub properly. As one of the team started chest compressions, I pulled on my gown and gloves and went into autopilot. The consultant still hadn't arrived. 'Knife.' The scrub nurse passed it to me. I looked at the anaesthetist. 'Are we good to go?'

'She's all yours.'

Taking a big breath, I sliced through her abdomen, reached deep inside, felt for the stomach, put my hand above it and pushed down hard. After a few moments, her heart started beating and the consultant walked through the door.

'OK?'

'Just about.'

I stayed where I was until he got a clamp on the aorta, and then went to get properly scrubbed. I was buzzing. I'd saved someone's life. Maybe I could be a surgeon after all.

My annual appraisal was coming up and I had to decide what to specialise in. Over the year my surgical comfort zone had become smaller and smaller. If I hadn't seen an operation twenty or thirty times, I wasn't confident enough to do it by myself. In comparison, most of the other registrars seemed happy to give anything a go and wanted all the operative exposure they could get. I hated being on-call. I didn't like the uncertainty of not knowing what I was going to find in theatre or whether I was good enough to fix it.

What I *did* love was talking to patients and working out what was wrong with them. And when I knew what I was doing in theatre, in a calm, controlled environment, I did enjoy operating. I loved being part of a team coming together to make a difference in someone's life. I thought back to my time in breast surgery. It was now becoming a speciality in its own right. Newly advertised posts were now coming off the on-call rota. That meant as a consultant I would never have to get up in the middle of the night again.

I walked into the meeting ready to ask for my final three years to be in breast surgery, but the committee had other ideas. My logbook was pitiful compared to my peers'. A lot of my weeks on-call had been spent babysitting patients with diverticulitis and cholecystitis who didn't need an operation, while my colleagues spent their shifts doing endless bowel resections. I had to get my numbers up, otherwise I wouldn't be allowed to sit the exit exam and that meant another year of colorectal surgery. I knew they were right but it didn't make it any easier. I was going to be sent to Luton, which meant being even further away from Dermot.

A few days later, we were cooking in his kitchen when he told me that he loved me. I didn't know how to reply. I'd never been in love before and had no idea whether what I felt for Dermot was love or something else. I'd read countless articles telling me that I'd just know, but the surgeon in me needed a more precise answer. How would I know if I'd never felt it before? The following week, Dermot had an interview for a national role and we'd both worked hard prepping for it. I was on-call and was anxiously waiting for a text to tell me that he'd got the job. I was running down the stairs on my way to A&E when my phone pinged. He hadn't got it. I sank down on the stairs and began to cry. He deserved that job. I never wanted him to feel pain like that again. I texted him back. The magazines were right after all. When you know, you know.

Chapter 15

I knew that Luton had two female consultant colorectal surgeons but I wasn't expecting to find myself on an entirely female team. Both consultants and the other registrar were married with children and it was great to see that it was possible to have a family and a surgical career. My consultant, Jenny, had been on the same training scheme as Dermot. She was delighted to hear that I was going out with him and quickly became a mentor, a confidante and a friend.

Before each theatre list started, we often had an hour to kill while the first patient was collected from the wards and the anaesthetists put all their lines in. One morning I'd just made us a cup of tea when I realised I'd forgotten to see a patient.

'Where are you going?' Jenny asked.

'I forgot to see that lady on the medical ward.'

'She can wait. The patient on the table is the only thing you should be thinking about. It's why I never go back to my office to do admin while I'm waiting for the list to start.'

I made a silent vow that I would do the same when I was a consultant.

The on-calls weren't as busy as Norwich but they were a lot more uncomfortable, mainly because there wasn't an on-call room for the registrars. We had to make do with our office instead. A lumpy plastic mattress was stored under the desk. If I didn't lie on that, it was the floor – a dark, wiry carpet covered in food stains and hair. I would borrow a blanket from the ward, use my handbag as a pillow and that was my bed for the night.

Luton was the regional bariatric centre and did a lot of surgery to help morbidly obese patients lose weight. As a consequence, emergency patients from other hospitals were often transferred there. Some of them had paid for surgery in Europe, presumably to avoid the waiting list in the UK, and now had complications. There was a separate bay on the wards for the patients requiring extra-large beds and chairs, and theatres had a special table to cope with the extra weight. I found it incredibly difficult to assess the patients for post-operative complications like a leak or perforation. Normally I would gently palpate someone's abdomen looking for rebound tenderness or guarding in one spot, but in bariatric patients these signs were almost impossible to pick up. The only thing I could go on to confirm that something had gone wrong was a fast heart rate. One night, a young twenty-three-year-old patient suddenly crashed on the ward. She'd had a gastric bypass the day before and was in a lot of pain. Her pulse was racing. I rang the on-call consultant. We ended up taking her back to theatre but she died a few days later on intensive care.

I tried hard to understand what life must be like for these patients. I knew obesity was a complex problem and there were no easy answers. It wasn't my place to judge, but I would often get frustrated when an overweight relative used the lift instead of walking down two flights of stairs. What did upset me, though, was the children. One night I had to do an appendicectomy on a twelve-year-old girl. She was only five feet tall and weighed over one hundred kilograms. I had to use the bariatric laparoscopic ports to look inside her abdomen.

That same night I had another appendicectomy to do but this time it was in a woman who was thirty-two weeks pregnant. I'd never done an operation on a pregnant woman before and neither had the consultant on-call. I'm not sure who was more nervous, him or me. The anatomy was all in the wrong place thanks to the baby. An obstetrician was standing by and a midwife came to monitor the baby's heartbeat. It was impossible to do it laparoscopically. The camera was normally inserted through the belly button but hers was now lying on top of the uterus. Instead of making a small cut near her right hip bone, I went in where she was most sore, just beneath her ribcage. Sure enough, an inflamed appendix was hiding there, having been pushed up and out of the way. It was the most surreal thing to see a foot kicking against the wall of the womb while I worked. Word must have spread because I did another three appendicectomies in pregnant women before I left. The consultants would call me for help because I'd seen so many.

December was a strange month. I had thought that the wards would be empty of elective cases, but one man in his fifties had asked to have his cancer surgery just before Christmas instead of waiting until it was over. After I'd finished consenting him for the surgery, I asked, 'Why did you choose to have surgery tomorrow instead of next week? Hospital Christmas dinners aren't that good, you know.'

'I wanted some peace and quiet,' he said. 'My family are treating me like an invalid. This way, I avoid all the usual drama too.'

It made sense. His Christmas had been ruined by a cancer diagnosis and now he didn't have to pretend to be happy for everyone else's sake.

The same week, a young mother of two had come in with severe abdominal pain on the overnight take. Jenny and I couldn't work out what was going on. Her X-rays and CT scan were essentially normal. After a couple of days, she still wasn't settling and we decided to take her to theatre for an exploratory laparotomy. It was Christmas Eve and I hoped it would be something simple like an adhesion. I opened her up, and we both looked inside. We looked at each other. Jenny's eyes had watered over and a tear rolled down my cheek. The peritoneum lining her abdomen was covered in thousands of tiny tumour deposits from a rare form of stomach cancer. There was nothing we could do. Jenny looked down and closed her eyes for a moment before asking for a looped nylon suture.

Everyone in the room knew what that meant. We were closing. The room fell silent while we stitched her up as neatly as we could. Happy Christmas. I was a mess when I got home that night. Life could be so cruel. Two young children were about to lose their mum. It was hard to think about baking mince pies and wrapping presents when my patient lay dying in a hospital bed.

———

Although I loved working with Jenny, I still wasn't certain that surgery was the right career for me. She could tell that something was up. One day over a colectomy she asked, 'Are you sure you want to be a surgeon?'

'I don't know anymore.'

'There are other options, you know. You don't even have to be a doctor.'

'I can't quit. It would mean I've wasted the last sixteen years of my life. I'd feel like a failure.'

'It's not a failure if it wasn't meant to be. Failing would mean carrying on when it doesn't make you happy. What do you like about surgery?'

'Problem-solving. Talking to patients. Being part of a team. Most of all, I just want to help people.'

'You don't need to be a surgeon to do that.'

'I know. It's easier now I have Dermot and a life outside of work. I've spent hours looking at other options and none of them appeal.'

'Do you think breast surgery will make you happy?'

'I think so. I like the patients. I like the operating. It's less stressful. There's no on-call. I could start to do things with my life again.'

'Well, OK then. Let's get your logbook up to scratch.'

At my annual appraisal the committee were finally happy for me to sit the exit exam and spend the next two years doing breast surgery. They were sending me to Ipswich, where I would be working for another two female consultants. The added bonus was that I could move in with Dermot.

Dermot, meanwhile, was planning to leave me for two months to sail the Northwest Passage with a couple of friends. In the heat of the summer he was busy buying thick waterproof sailing suits and thermal underwear to cope with the ice in the Arctic. He asked me to marry him the weekend before he left. My life was slowly falling into place.

The day he flew off to the Arctic, I bought my first wedding magazine. I'd planned to read it in the bath with a glass of wine. As I took my bra off, I felt a lump in my left breast. It was round and firm to touch. I felt sick to my stomach. As I went back downstairs, my head was spinning. I was convinced it was breast cancer. I'd need chemotherapy. I couldn't wear a wedding dress with no breasts and no hair. Would Dermot still want to marry me? I'd be dead in a year. All rational thought had gone out the window. It was too late to call my mum. I lay on the sofa and howled. My life was over.

I tried to appear normal in theatre but Jenny wasn't fooled. I told her I was just missing Dermot. At the end of the morning list we walked back to her office and I couldn't keep it in any longer. Bursting into tears, I said, 'I've found a breast lump.'

'So that's what's been going on. Let's see if we can get you into the breast clinic this afternoon.'

Jenny pulled some strings and they were able to squeeze me in. I felt so embarrassed being examined by one of the consultants I worked with but he was incredibly professional. He told me I had very lumpy breasts and that it was probably a cyst. I went next door to have an ultrasound, too scared to look at the screen.

'It's just a cyst,' said the radiologist.

'Is that normal?' I asked.

'It is for a woman of your age.'

I let out a huge sigh of relief. 'You're certain it's not cancer?'

'Yes,' she said. 'Your breasts are full of cysts. Have a look for yourself.'

I turned to look at the screen and saw lots of tiny black holes in a cloud of grey.

'A cancer looks very different.'

The last month at Luton flew by. I'd actually enjoyed operating again and it was all due to Jenny. I was sad to leave her. She'd kept me going when Dermot was away and had helped me realise I did still want to be a surgeon. She'd patiently coached and coaxed me every step of the way, and I was now certain that a career in breast surgery would make me happy. It was time to move on, move in with Dermot, and plan our wedding.

Chapter 16

I couldn't wait to do breast surgery again and hoped I would love it enough to specialise as a consultant. I was going to be working for Amanda, who had only been a consultant herself for a few years. There were four breast care nurses and one of them, Sally, became a good friend, partly because neither of us had children. It was great to have someone to talk to when everyone else was chatting about exams and birthday parties.

I thought I knew what to expect from the job, having done it twice before, but I couldn't have been more wrong. The speciality had undergone significant changes. Amanda was an oncoplastic breast surgeon and used plastic surgical skills to reshape, re-drape and recreate a breast. The slash-and-grab mastectomies now belonged in the past and I had strange new words to learn like mammoplasty and mastopexy.

The first case I did with Amanda was a woman in her sixties with a large cancer in an even larger breast. She was having a therapeutic mammoplasty. I knew it was like a breast reduction but that was the extent of my knowledge.

'Why isn't she having a mastectomy?' I asked.

'If the cancer takes up more than twenty per cent of the breast volume,' said Amanda, 'there isn't enough tissue to reshape the breast and give a decent cosmetic result. If a woman has small breasts, she has to have a mastectomy or a reconstruction. However, if her breasts are large, like this lady, you can remove the cancer as part of a breast reduction. It takes longer to do but the end result is worth it.'

I watched her mark up the patient. She pulled out a tape measure from her bag, draped it around the woman's neck and drew the new nipple position. Then she pushed the breasts left and right, drawing a keyhole anchor pattern to mark how much skin and tissue would need to be removed. It was more like advanced dress making than surgical marking.

After we'd scrubbed, Amanda encircled one breast with both hands, stretching the skin until it was taut. 'Off you go', she said.

'You want me to start?'

'You've got to learn how to do this. Get a blade and start stripping.'

I started to peel away the top layer of skin inside the area she had marked. I felt like I was filleting a fish as I slowly worked my way over the breast. Amanda then took me through the principles of the cancer surgery, showing me how much I could remove while keeping a good blood supply to the tissue left behind. Once she'd done the reduction, the breast looked like a bombsite.

'Now the magic happens.' She tacked it back together, joining up the lines we'd made earlier and creating a new hole for the nipple. It looked like a breast again.

'That's amazing,' I said.

'Isn't it? Right. On to the other side. Your turn.'

Once I'd finished, Amanda went to the end of the bed and asked the anaesthetist to sit the patient up. 'We need to check she's symmetrical before we close', she said. It felt so crude to stare at the woman's breasts, eyeballing them and asking everyone else in theatre what they thought.

We spent the next hour painstakingly suturing the skin. I was starving by the time we'd finished. The operation had taken over three hours but I hadn't noticed the time. I was transfixed by this new world of oncoplastic surgery and the possibilities that lay ahead.

The first case on the afternoon list was a simple lumpectomy. I got ready to cut down over the lump when Amanda stopped me.

'What are you doing?' she asked.

'What I normally do.'

'Not anymore. You never leave a visible scar on the breast if you can help it.'

She took the scalpel and cut between the areola and the breast. She tunnelled under the skin until she could feel the cancer under her fingers before cutting down to the chest wall to remove it. Finally, she tacked the breast tissue back together to close the gap before neatly suturing the skin. The scar was barely visible on the edge of the nipple. For the second time that day, my mind was blown.

The next week I got to sit in with Amanda in clinic while she measured a patient for an implant. She was having a reconstruction the following week. With her trusty tape measure, Amanda recorded the height, depth and width of each breast to work out what size implants to order. It was like a dark art. I couldn't wait to see the surgery. In theatre, she cut around the nipple and carefully separated the skin from the tissue underneath until the whole of the breast was free. It looked incredibly awkward as she peered into the dark cavity trying to see around the mound.

'That looks really difficult to do,' I said.

'It is,' Amanda replied. 'But it's the most important part of the operation. If the flaps are too thin, there's a risk that the skin will necrose because it's not getting enough blood. If they're too thick, you might leave breast tissue behind, which increases the risk of recurrence.'

'It's a bit like Goldilocks, isn't it?' I said.

She then completed the mastectomy, peeling the breast off the chest wall like a satsuma.

'Guess how much it weighs.'

I had no idea.

'The more you do it,' she said, 'the better you get at implant sizing. I'll go first. I reckon it's three hundred and seventy grams.'

Everyone else in the room joined in until I was the only one left to guess. I weighed it in both hands, trying to remember what a bag of sugar felt like. 'I'm going with three hundred.'

One of the theatre assistants placed it on the scales.

'It's three hundred and sixty-five. Amanda wins. Loser buys the cake when we stop for coffee. Liz, that's you.'

'OK, we'll open the three-sixty implant,' said Amanda. 'Is the mesh ready?'

The scrub nurse passed it to her. Amanda stitched it to the chest wall where the bottom of the breast used to be, creating a sling to hold the implant. She lifted the pectoral muscle and draped it over the top. I sutured the muscle and mesh together, covering the implant completely. We went down to the end of the bed to check our handiwork. Both breasts looked almost identical in size and shape. Instead of having a mastectomy, this woman would leave hospital with two breasts. I couldn't believe that I would soon have the power to offer this to my own patients.

Instead of staying overnight, most patients now went home on the same day as their surgery. The only people who were kept in were those women having a reduction or reconstruction. It meant I had no patients to look after on the wards, and most of my time was spent in clinic.

Most cases were fairly straightforward. I was back to reassuring women with breast pain that they didn't have cancer and telling them to go shopping for a bra that fitted properly. One day I saw a young woman in her thirties. She'd had a cough for a couple of months and was exhausted but she'd put it down to looking after her young twins. I had a bad feeling about her and could feel a large lump at the back of her breast. Her armpit was full of enlarged nodes. I ordered a mammogram and a chest X-ray and arranged to see her the following week with the results. It wasn't good. She had breast cancer that had spread to her bones and lungs. Amanda offered to tell her but I wanted to. I'd have to do it as a consultant and this way I could talk to Amanda afterwards about how it went.

It was going to be the first time I would tell someone they had incurable breast cancer. Sally brought the patient into the room and my heart sank. She looked worse than before and now had to lean on her husband for support as she sat down. I could tell by the look in her eyes that she knew what was coming. I did it as gently as I could. Sally and I left them alone to come to terms with the news in private. I went into the doctor's room, sat down and said, 'It's not fair.'

'I know,' Amanda said.

Sally came in with biscuits and we sat in silence, readying ourselves before going to tell the next woman she had cancer.

Halfway through the year, Amanda moved to work at West Suffolk. A lot of consultants moved after a couple of years and she was looking forward to introducing oncoplastic surgery to the unit. I was gutted when she left, but on the positive side it meant that there would be a job coming up in Ipswich.

Before I could worry about where I was going to work as a consultant, I had the small matter of the exit exam to pass. I paid the £1,700 fee and steadily worked my way through an ever-growing list of textbooks. A friend told me to wear pearls to the exam. She'd been given the tip by one of her female bosses. The theory was that they made the old men examining you think you were like their daughter and go easy on you. My mum lent me her pearls and I hoped my friend was right.

The anteroom where they kept us waiting was a mass of nerves and desperation. Everyone was frantically skimming through folders of notes and textbooks. I'd brought my own cramming list but I couldn't focus. The invigilator lined us up and directed us to our first viva. I recognised the faces of previous bosses and hoped that I wouldn't end up opposite one of them. I couldn't take the pressure of potentially messing up in front of someone I'd worked with. Thankfully all my examiners were strangers and I managed to answer every question. I had five oral exams that day and two clinical exams the next. In two weeks' time, I would know whether I'd done enough. When the results letter finally arrived, I was too scared to open it. I begged Dermot to do it for me but he refused. With a deep breath I ripped it open. I'd passed.

There was only one more hurdle left to jump. I wanted to get a national oncoplastic fellowship. Breast surgery was a small speciality and consultant posts didn't come up very often. The competition could be fierce and the extra training would give me an edge. The fellowship was unique because there were no fixed ward or clinic commitments. It was up to each fellow to design a timetable to fill in the gaps in their training. If successful, I would work closely with both breast and plastic surgeons, learning how to do more advanced procedures and manage complex patients. The icing on the cake was that there were no on-calls.

Twelve of us were interviewed for nine jobs so the odds were in my favour. The problem was that the units were scattered all over the country. If I was the last to be appointed, I could get sent to a hospital hundreds of miles away from home. Thankfully, my interview preparation paid off and I got my first-choice placement at the

Royal Marsden Hospital in London. It meant I could live with Dermot's parents during the week and commute back and forth by train at the weekends.

I started counting down the days until my last-ever on-call shift. It had been a busy week of nights and the only thing keeping me going was the knowledge that I would never have to do it again. I dragged myself to the admissions unit for the final handover and was met by a very stressed SHO. She hadn't seen the registrar all day as he'd been operating. There were nine urgent cases that needed reviewing. It was going to take me most of the night and that was before I took into account any new admissions. My bleep went off.

'Can you come up and take over from Ahmed so he can go home? We're in theatre eight.'

That was the colorectal theatre, not the emergency theatre. What was going on? Only one way to find out. Ahmed and one of the colorectal consultants had their hands deep inside a woman's abdomen. I slipped in beside him and took hold of the retractor he was holding. I looked into the abdomen and swore. All I could see was a grey cocoon in her pelvis. She'd obviously had several previous operations. A mass of adhesions had formed around her bowel, causing an obstruction, and every strand needed to be carefully divided. It was going to take hours.

Ahmed turned to me and said, 'Thanks for coming up so quickly. Sorry I haven't seen any of the cases from the day. There was an appendix booked but it's been postponed until tomorrow. I don't think there's anything else brewing on the wards but I'll have a quick scan before I go.'

It took another three hours for us to finish. I could feel the collective sigh of relief from the theatre staff as we pulled off the drapes at the end of the case. Time for a much-needed cup of tea. Then I looked at my bleep and saw the list of messages that had piled up for me. Before I had a chance to read them, it went off again. It was A&E.

'There's a ninety-two-year-old lady with a probable saddle embolus.'

'I'm on my way.'

A saddle embolus is a vascular emergency. A large clot forms at the bottom of the aorta, blocking blood flow to the legs. I needed to find out if she was fit enough to have an operation to remove it. When I arrived, her legs were already cold. There was no time to lose. She was otherwise fit and well and only took an aspirin at night. I looked at the clock. Half-past midnight. Time to ring the vascular consultant and explain.

'Is she a goer?' he asked.

'I think she is.'

'OK, I'll see you in theatre.'

Half an hour later I was scrubbed again. There was something rather magical about watching the consultant pull out the long black clot. After a few tense moments I could feel the pulses in her feet. We'd got there in time to save her legs. The consultant de-scrubbed to start writing up the notes, leaving me to close the wounds. I glanced at the clock. It was now 2.30 a.m. There was another pile of messages on my bleep.

It had gone three by the time I finished. I pushed open the scrub room door to see the general surgical consultant rush past me. He was closely followed by an anaesthetist pushing a young man on a trolley lying on his side clutching his abdomen.

'We've got a stabbing.'

The patient looked like he'd been bitten by a shark. There was a huge hole between his right ribcage and hip bone with a bloody wound pad covering it and bowel peeking out.

I followed them into theatre. As my boss extended the wound through the abdominal muscles, a litre of blood poured on to the floor followed by most of the small bowel. Someone threw absorbent pads by our feet to stop us slipping and we carried on. There was a huge haematoma in the mesentery of the bowel where the knife had gone in and his colon had also been damaged.

We did a resection and then I walked the bowel, passing every inch through my fingers looking for nicks, tears and bleeding points. I couldn't see anything else but the anaesthetist wasn't happy. She was convinced he was still bleeding. After another careful look inside I found a boggy area at the back of the abdominal cavity. The knife must have gone through the peritoneum into the kidney. We flipped him back on to his side, opened up the retroperitoneum and removed another litre of blood clot. There was a deep gash in the kidney but luckily the knife had missed the ureter. I hadn't seen a kidney in real life since my early days of paediatric surgery. Inside I was panicking but the consultant took it all in his stride as he calmly repaired it.

After putting the final staple in the wound and covering it with a dressing, I was drained. I desperately needed a cup of tea. The bloody scrubs were stuck to my legs and I could feel cold clots of blood in my shoes. I looked at the clock. It was eight in the morning. I'd been operating all night. My last night of on-call and I'd seen everything: colorectal surgery, vascular surgery, trauma and urology. It was the perfect farewell to my general surgical training.

Chapter 17

Starting the fellowship was bittersweet. I was excited to spend a year learning from some of the best surgeons in the country but having to leave Dermot the week before our wedding and spend the next year living apart was hard to do. His parents were lovely and at least I was living with people I knew. Some of the other fellows weren't as lucky. The fellowship came with a fifty per cent pay cut because there was no on-call. Commuting and renting weren't cheap. It was the sacrifice we all made to become a better surgeon.

The first week was a blur as I made my way around the maze that was the Marsden introducing myself to the breast and plastic surgeons. I had the luxury of being able to pick which clinics and lists I went to and there were a lot to choose from. It was going to take some time to work out how to fit everything in but I had the small matter of getting married first.

The ceremony was in an ancient church on the Norfolk coast followed by a reception in the small hotel where Dermot had taken me for our first weekend away together. We'd secretly been having dance lessons to surprise our guests when the band played our song, and I couldn't have wished for a more perfect day. Dermot had planned the honeymoon. All I knew was that I needed to pack for sunshine, snow and everything in between. I had no idea where we were going. The first flight was with Iberian Airlines and I briefly thought he was taking me to Ibiza, but then we flew out of Madrid into Buenos Aires and spent three wonderful weeks touring Argentina, Brazil and Chile. I didn't want it to end.

Back at the Marsden, I found out that I wasn't the first O'Riordan to work for Louise, the senior breast surgeon. Dermot had been her registrar many years ago. It was a privilege to watch her work. Her clinics were often full of women who'd come for second and third opinions clutching copies of scientific papers they'd found online, desperate for someone to tell them what they wanted to hear. Sadly, they rarely heard it. Breast surgery is practised according to guidelines based on trials involving hundreds of thousands of women over many years. It's unusual for anyone to practise outside these guidelines.

One morning we saw a woman in her forties for her third opinion who had been diagnosed with cancer six months before. So far she'd turned down every treatment. Her GP was hoping that Louise could persuade her to have surgery. The small cancer found at diagnosis was now taking up most of her breast and I could feel a mass of hard, enlarged lymph nodes in her armpit that were clinically 'involved'. It's another way of saying that the nodes are cancerous. Louise sat down next to her and asked, 'Why you don't want to have surgery?'

'I don't need it,' she said. 'Jesus is going to save me.

This is a test so I can show him how much I love him. The strength of my prayers will see me through.'

I had no idea what to say. I'd never heard anyone turn down treatment for religious reasons. Louise stepped in. 'I can see that your faith is very important to you. It will help you cope with whatever lies ahead, but it can't save you from this. Your cancer is growing and has started to spread. Without surgery, it will kill you.'

I had heard previous bosses be that honest before, but I had never witnessed it with such compassion and kindness. The patient looked at Louise in shock. It was obviously the first time a doctor had told her what would happen if she didn't have surgery. She started to cry. 'I'm scared,' she said.

Louise held her hand. 'I know. You're going to need the support of your church more than ever, but you need to let me treat you.'

Once the patient had left, I asked Louise if it had been hard to say.

'Not really. I'm just telling the truth. What's hard is knowing that the other surgeons she saw didn't do their job. Her cancer has obviously grown and she's got a worse chance of survival. We have to tell patients what they need to hear, even if it might upset them.' I learned a lot that day.

In theatre I was like a child in a sweetshop, being able to jump from one reconstruction to the next. If a woman didn't want or wasn't suitable for an implant, she was offered a reconstruction using her abdominal fat called a DIEP flap, after the deep inferior epigastric perforator vessels that kept the tissue alive. The plastic surgeons removed the fat from the stomach en bloc and the flap's tiny artery and vein were plumbed into vessels on the chest wall once the breast had been removed. It was my job to do the mastectomies for the plastic surgeons. During one list, Justin, the consultant, asked me, 'Do you have a portfolio of your own photographs?'

'No,' I said.

'You need one. It's important to be able to show patients your results. It's vital that any woman I consent knows exactly what to expect. Never show patients the photos of your best results. I start with the few cases where I didn't get it right first time. If she's on board with that, then she'll be delighted with the end result.'

'That makes sense,' I said.

'Then show them photos of your complications. There are so many factors that can affect how it looks at the end – the quality of her skin, how much fat there is, the thickness of the flaps. If you promise her perfection, she'll be disappointed.'

I added a photo album to the growing list of things I was going to do once I became a consultant.

A few weeks later, Louise was teaching me how to do a nipple reconstruction. Although lots of women were happy with just a nipple tattoo, which gave incredibly realistic results, some wanted surgery to create one. I watched as Louise lifted a small flap of skin and fat along the central scar on the breast. She folded it to create a tiny tube with a hat before suturing it to create a nipple. It was like origami.

'You'd think everyone would want it,' I said.

'Don't be so sure. One of my old registrars saw a patient

in clinic, similar to this lady, at a follow-up appointment. After examining her, he said, "Your reconstruction looks really good. Now all you need is a nipple on it." I got a complaint a few days later. She'd been delighted with the surgery and was happy with how she looked. After hearing what he said to her, she now felt ugly and hated it. Never assume anything.'

When I wasn't working with Louise or the plastic surgeons, I sometimes got the chance to sit in with Charles, the other breast consultant, in clinic. He was referred a lot of young women with a BRCA gene mutation who wanted a bilateral mastectomy and reconstruction. The gene mutation meant that they had a very high chance of getting breast cancer in their lifetime, somewhere between sixty and eighty per cent. While many women opted for regular scans, some chose to have surgery. The stakes were much higher as this was essentially a cosmetic operation. In order to give a better outcome, Charles did a nipple-sparing mastectomy. Instead of removing the nipple to get access, he cut underneath the breast, tunnelling up and over to remove it. It was technically challenging, but the results were worth it.

The women had to go through rounds of counselling to make sure they knew what they were signing up for, and that continued in the surgical clinics. One woman in her twenties had come with her mum, who'd been treated for breast cancer the previous year. She was excited at the thought of being able to have larger breasts with the implants. Charles had to let her down gently. 'The reason we're doing the surgery is to try and stop you getting breast cancer in the future,' he said. 'There's always a very small risk that you'll get a complication meaning that the implants have to be removed and you're left with a flat chest. You have to be mentally prepared to accept that.' Charles continued, 'You also need to remember that your breasts and nipples will be numb. The skin loses sensation when I remove the underlying tissue. You won't feel anything when a future partner touches them, and you won't be able to breastfeed if you have children.'

'I hadn't thought of that,' she said.

'That's why many women choose to have the scans instead. You've got to be one hundred per cent certain that you want to go through this.' Charles gave her another appointment to see the psychologist and told her to take her time.

The year of commuting was starting to take its toll. My Friday-night train didn't get in until ten and while Dermot was excited to see me, I was exhausted and just wanted to sleep. We tried to make an effort on the Saturdays when he wasn't on-call, but it was hard. I was irritable and the slightest thing annoyed me. Sundays were spent counting down the hours until I had to get back on a train again. Although I loved the training that the fellowship provided, my marriage was suffering and I couldn't wait for the year to be over.

My final appraisal was stressful because I didn't have a job to go to when the fellowship finished. After spending all this time training, I could still be unemployed at the end. I'd kept in touch with Amanda and she came up with a solution. West Suffolk were going to be one registrar short for the next six months because of maternity leave and she suggested that I work for her. It would mean doing on-calls again but it would be worth it to see Dermot every day. Thankfully, the Deanery agreed and they gave me a six-month grace period to find a consultant post.

It felt like coming home. I didn't enjoy being on-call again, but it was generally quiet. When I did get called about a patient, Dermot would wake up too and I had an automatic second opinion right beside me. It was strange operating with him again in theatre. We had to be professional and act like consultant and registrar, not husband and wife. The flirting and teasing were saved for the corridors and the coffee room.

Dermot had started cycling to work and joined the local cycling club. He'd introduced me to the Tour de France over the summer, and I was hooked. I'd gone from someone who had no interest in sport to screaming at the TV hoping my favourite rider would win the stage. Dermot bought me a bike for Christmas and, after putting on all the layers, we ventured out for our first ride together. After an hour or so, we stopped next to a church in one of the local villages so I could have a drink. I was a long way off mastering the art of drinking on the go. I asked Dermot, 'How far are we going?'

'Let me know when you're halfway tired and we'll turn around.'

'How on earth do I know when I'm halfway tired if I don't know how far I'm going?'

He couldn't understand why his suggestion made no sense at all. It is true when they say that opposites attract.

———

Within a few months I'd swapped my trainers for bike shoes and clip-in pedals and we'd signed up for a local fifty-mile ride. I'd never done anything like it before and was scared when I found myself surrounded by hundreds of other riders. Dermot dragged me up and down every hill and, to top it all, we both got a medal at the end. It was now all about the bling, and I started looking for other rides I could do.

Finally, the Ipswich job was advertised. The interview was hard but I thought I'd presented myself well. I was told to stay in the hospital and that someone would phone me to let me know. I managed to find a table in the café and sat there nursing a cup of tea. Half an hour had passed and I started to worry. I was the last candidate to be interviewed. If it was taking this long to decide then there was a real chance I wouldn't get the job. The café filled up with visitors and I felt bad for taking up a table, so I moved to the outpatient waiting area and flicked through an out-of-date magazine. After another half an hour my phone finally rang. I felt sick to my stomach as I made my way back. One of the other candidates was already there and I sat down next to him, wiping my sweaty palms on my suit.

They called me in first and told me that the panel couldn't decide between the two of us so they'd created an extra job instead. I was in shock. I was so certain I was going to hear I'd been unsuccessful. I shook hands with everyone and thanked them, desperate to get out of the room and text Dermot. The news started to sink in. It had taken twenty years but I had finally made it. I was going to be a consultant breast surgeon.

Chapter 18

The day had finally arrived. I was about to fulfil the promise I made when I accompanied my dad on his ward rounds all those years ago. As I looked at my new name badge, I realised no one would ever train me again. My stabilisers had been removed and it was time to ride solo.

It was such a special moment when I walked into theatre as a consultant for the first time and introduced myself to the team. I'd worked with most of them before when I was a registrar and we just clicked. I had two amazing scrub nurses, Chris and Val, who always had my back. There was music and laughter, and my operating list quickly became my favourite time of the week.

It was such a privilege to take a patient through an operation as they placed their trust and their life in my hands. I was now ultimately responsible for their care, and I desperately wanted to protect them all. I enjoyed being able to plan how I was going to remove each cancer without leaving a scar. It was so good to see the look on a patient's face when their dressings came off. One evening I'd stopped at a supermarket on the way home to pick up something to eat and a woman came up to me in the aisle.

'Look,' she said. And then she flashed me.

I didn't recognise her face, but I knew her breasts. There was a faint blue mark near her right nipple where I'd injected the dye.

'Thank you, doctor,' she said. 'I had to show you. I show everyone. They can't believe I've had surgery.'

My anaesthetist, Keith, was brilliant with the patients. One morning I was doing a mastectomy on a sprightly lady in her nineties using local anaesthetic. She'd come to theatre with a full face of make-up and was a real character. I could hear Keith laughing as he chatted. Once I was finished, I removed the screen shielding her from my handiwork and said, 'We're all done.'

'Really? That was so quick.'

'I'm impressed that you're wearing make-up this early in the morning,' I said. 'I love your lipstick.'

'My mother always told me to never leave the house without foundation and powder on.'

Keith said, 'She was a wise woman. I must say, you've got fantastic skin.'

She beckoned Keith to lean in closer and said, 'I'll let you in on my secret. All I use is Nivea Cold Cream. You could do with some yourself. And tomato juice. Drink lots of tomato juice.'

Keith couldn't stop laughing as he wheeled her through to recovery. Guess what I got him for Christmas?

It wasn't all plain sailing, though. My first reconstruction couldn't have been in a more technically challenging patient. She was slim with large breasts and wanted to keep her nipples. I struggled to find an implant that would fit, and I was worried that she wouldn't have a good match afterwards. The surgery was difficult, but I was pleased with the results and I couldn't wait to see her in clinic once everything had healed. The look on her face as she walked into the room told me everything.

'You've ruined my life,' she said. 'The nipple on the implant side is five millimetres higher. I look awful. I can never let my husband see me naked again.'

I didn't know what to say. I thought she'd got a brilliant result and was eager to get photographs so I could show future patients, but she refused. She stormed out of the room threatening to sue me. I needed to find a better way of helping patients know what to expect after surgery. I remembered what Louise used to say when she was consenting women. Breasts are sisters, not twins; no pair is identical. I would use that phrase from now on.

Outside of theatre, most of my time was spent in clinics and they always overran. We were allotted ten minutes per patient, but it just wasn't enough. I started every consultation with an apology, hoping it would calm down those who'd been waiting for over an hour. The unit was blessed with a couple of amazing volunteers who made hot drinks for everyone in the waiting room. I called them the tea fairies, and I couldn't have done my job without them.

It was even harder to break bad news now that I was responsible for everything, and I often felt like I was being paid to make women cry. Every Friday I had the pleasure of doing this back-to-back. I called it double maths. The morning started with a results clinic in the oncology unit and most of the time it was good news. Happy faces with well-healed scars, clear margins and negative nodes. I started getting thank-you presents. Bunches of flowers and boxes of chocolates that were shared with the rest of the team. But some days, it was all bad. Women with positive lymph nodes who now needed chemotherapy. Women with involved margins who had to have more surgery. Women with a cancer much larger than expected, meaning a greater risk of recurrence and death.

In the second clinic I got to tell women that their biopsies were positive. Although most took it in their stride, a few ran out of the room crying before returning an hour later. There were those who crumpled as they remembered their own mother dying of the disease and those paralysed by the fear that they would pass it on to their own daughters. Those frightened that their husbands would leave them when they only had one breast and those who simply got out their phone and asked when the operation would be so they could put it in their calendar. It wasn't just the women I had to deal with, but their partners too. Some fainted, some punched the desk, one tried to punch me. This was my going to be my life for the next twenty-five years. Breaking women in clinic and trying to rebuild them in theatre before going home and turning into a wife. Consultants didn't get counselling. We were just expected to cope.

If Dermot and I had both had tough days, it was a race to speak first. If he won, he got to unburden while I listened. I didn't have the energy to talk about my day afterwards. And while his tough days were few and far between, mine were as regular as clockwork. I couldn't spend every Friday night telling him about all the women I'd seen. Instead, I simply stopped talking about work. I didn't want to bring cancer into my marriage.

We still cycled most weekends and had signed up to do the Ride 100 in August. It was a new one-hundred-mile event around London. I'd only ever ridden fifty miles before, but I was up for the challenge. I swore at my phone when the alarm went off at four in the morning. I had to force breakfast down but then we were off, riding through the backstreets as dawn was breaking on our way to the start line. There were thousands of cyclists lined up with music blaring and a real buzz in the air. It was surreal to be cheered on by huge crowds of people. I felt famous as I whizzed past them, grinning from ear to ear. Dermot dragged me up the hills as usual and after seven and a half hours we crossed the finish line. The medal was really big, and I couldn't wait to do it again the following year. But something was missing. I needed an activity that was mine. I used to swim a lot at school, and because I'd done the London Marathon I started investigating the world of triathlon. I pored over every magazine I could find until Dermot got fed up and entered me into a race just before my fortieth birthday the following year.

In September I found another lump in my left breast. I was sure it was another cyst but it didn't stop me worrying. My GP asked me where I wanted to be seen. I didn't want my own team talking about me in a meeting, so I asked her to send me to Amanda at West Suffolk. I sat in the waiting room with everyone else, getting a new perspective on what it was like for women while they waited to see me. Thankfully, the mammogram was normal, and it was just another cyst.

Back at work I was trying not to get emotionally involved with my patients. One afternoon I had to see a young woman in her twenties who'd found a lump when trying on her wedding dress. She had metastatic cancer and couldn't be cured. There was no time to take a break and compose myself as there were still another six patients left to see. Instead, I fixed my smudged mascara, plastered a smile on my face and put on the mask. The next patient needed me at my best and this was the only way I could do it.

The breast unit ran a flexible timetable, which meant I wasn't always able to follow a patient through from diagnosis to discharge. Continuity of care was so important to me and it was frustrating when I couldn't offer it. Still, looking after patients was the easy part. It was everything else that was hard. I had been trained to be a surgeon, but I hadn't been shown how to lead a team or run a business. It was the steepest learning curve that I'd ever experienced. I had no idea how to write a business case to ask for a new piece of surgical equipment. I naïvely thought that you just asked theatres and they ordered it for you.

I also didn't know how to deal with complaints. The first one I got was from a woman who'd had a lumpectomy over a year ago. She was still exhausted after the radiotherapy and angry that I hadn't told her it might happen. Although I normally touched on the side effects, it was the oncologists who covered them in more detail. It was going to take some time for her notes to be pulled from medical records and I didn't want to keep her waiting for a reply. Instead, I contacted the complaints department and asked if I could meet her in person to apologise.

I was very nervous before going into the room. A lady from the complaints team was sitting next to my patient with a copy of the letter in her hand.

'Thank you for meeting me,' I said. 'I can't imagine how difficult this is for you, but I wanted to apologise in person and see if there's anything I can do to help.'

She told me that she'd never wanted radiotherapy and had since found out that if she'd had a mastectomy, she could have avoided it. I was stunned. It had never occurred to me that a patient would choose to have their breast removed to avoid radiotherapy. I'd always thought of it as a harmless treatment but maybe I was wrong. In team meetings we discussed women's scans and results before deciding on the best surgical option, always trying to save the breast where possible. I couldn't remember the last time I'd heard anyone say that a mastectomy was also an option if the patient wanted it. I promised myself that I would now offer a mastectomy to every woman I saw.

The hardest part about being a consultant, though, was the loneliness. I hadn't realised how isolating it was going to be. As a trainee I'd been surrounded by people I knew and there was always someone in the mess to talk to over lunch. Now when I did get a lunch break, I ate in the office alone while I caught up with admin. I tried the canteen once, but I didn't recognise anyone. I wasn't brave enough to sit down at a table with people I didn't know. Instead, I found an empty table right at the back and turned my seat to face the wall so no one would see me cry. After that, I started eating lunch in my car.

I often had different opinions about how to manage patients and it could be tough to get my voice across. I began to question my own clinical judgement. As the months went by I became less and less confident. The only place I felt safe was in theatre. It became my sanctuary but even that didn't last. My regular team were assigned to other lists. Chris and Val were replaced by different nurses every week. The camaraderie was gone.

I started having regular nightmares, two on rotation. In the first I was sitting an exam I hadn't revised for. In the second, my teeth kept falling out. It was so real that I had to get up and check they were still there. When my alarm did go off, I spent every waking moment trying to find an excuse not to go to work. I always went. I had to. I couldn't let my patients down. But it didn't stop me thinking. Could I fall off my bike on purpose? If I broke my collarbone, I'd need time off to recover. As I got closer to the hospital, my mind went into overdrive thinking about what I could do. I would count the minutes until I could get in the car to go home, but instead of feeling relief, I felt sick to my stomach that it would start all over again the following morning.

Spring finally arrived and I'd almost made it through my first year. I began to feel more positive as the bulbs in the garden started to bloom, but it didn't last. After a difficult morning telling four young mothers that they had cancer, I found out that my afternoon meeting had been cancelled. I jumped in the car, desperate to escape. Back home I kicked off my heels and padded into the kitchen to make a cup of tea. As I entered the kitchen and scanned the pile of papers lying in a heap on the worktop, I felt my heart stop for a second. A sense of panic flew over me as I briefly thought about doing something to end the pain I was in. As the kettle started to boil, I ran upstairs to the bedroom shutting every door between me and the kitchen to keep me safe until Dermot came home.

I woke up a few hours later when Dermot's car pulled into the drive, and forced myself to get out of bed and start cooking supper. I didn't say a word about what had nearly happened. I had the next day off and lied to Dermot about all the nice things I had no intention of doing.

I woke up the next morning and my heart started racing as I remembered what I'd almost done. I was scared. Was this more than just stress at work? Maybe I was depressed again. If I could persuade my GP to give me some antidepressants, I'd be back to my old self in no time. I booked an emergency appointment for later that afternoon.

I lost my nerve in the waiting room. I wasn't really ill and I didn't really need to be seen. I didn't want to waste anyone's time. Just as I was about to make a run for it, my name was called. My normal GP was doing the emergency clinic that day.

'What's going on?' he said.

'Nothing really. I know there's loads of people waiting to see you so I won't take up much of your time. I'm just a bit depressed, that's all.'

'Are you having trouble sleeping?

'Not really, but I've been getting regular nightmares.'

'I see. And when you're stressed, do your thoughts start racing?'

'Yes, but that's normal for me.'

'When did you last laugh?'

'At work? You must be joking. I'm a cancer surgeon. I spend my days making people cry.'

'And at home?'

I fell silent. I couldn't remember the last time. I curled forward in the chair, my eyes filling up with tears.

'There's more, isn't there?' he said.

'No,' I sniffed. 'I'm just a bit down. I don't want to waste your time. I know you're busy.'

'Forget about everyone else. This is an emergency appointment. There isn't a time limit.'

I couldn't pretend anymore. A floodgate opened and I told him everything, immediately regretting it.

'Honestly, I'm fine,' I said. 'I just need some tablets to get me through this rough patch.'

'You're telling me that you're safe to cut someone open after telling me you were suicidal. It doesn't add up.'

I had no answers. The truth was slowly sinking in. I saw myself through his eyes. A scared, frightened, vulnerable woman in need of help. We went around in circles. I was trying to bargain with him not to sign me off work, but he stuck to his guns. He signed me off for a month with stress so no one would know it was depression. I was grateful for that. I was so scared of anyone finding out. Especially my patients.

He handed me a prescription for citalopram, an antidepressant, and a phone number for the local mental health helpline.

As I got up to leave, he said, 'Go and spend this time doing something you're passionate about. Forget about work for a while.'

I stared out the kitchen window for hours as my cup of tea turned cold. I'd have given anything to swap places with the blackbird on the grass outside singing his heart out without a care in the world. I felt guilty for being depressed. I was lucky to have a wonderful husband, a good job, a stable income, a loving family. There were millions of people in far, far worse situations. I was ashamed of myself. I'd let my husband down. My parents down. Worse still, I'd let my patients down. I had failed at life.

When Dermot eventually came home from work, he asked me how my day had been. I resorted to those four little words that always spell trouble. 'We need to talk.'

He turned with a sigh and said, 'This can't be good.'

'I've been signed off work for a month with depression.'

I sat down and told him everything. It was a relief to get it all out in the open. He turned away from me for a moment and my heart cracked.

Dermot didn't say anything. Instead, he gave me the tightest hug. It was all I needed. At that moment, I knew that everything was going to be all right. I wriggled to lift my head and saw that I'd made him cry. He gave me a gentle kiss on the lips and hugged me again, nestling my head against his chest. I wanted to stay there forever with the warmth of the afternoon sun on our shoulders, but Chester was pacing around our feet demanding to be fed.

I knew Dermot would need time to come to terms with everything he'd just heard. We'd both been living a lie for the past six months, only he didn't know it. However, with that hug he'd shown me the promise of love and support for something he didn't yet understand. I knew he'd be there beside me, just like we'd said in our marriage vows – in sickness and in health.

Chapter 19

The next morning I plucked up the courage to call my mum. I'd been putting it off because I knew how upset she'd be. It was so hard hearing the pain in her voice. She wanted to know why I hadn't told her I was feeling down. I tried to explain that I didn't know how ill I'd become. I just thought I was stressed. We were both crying by the time I hung up.

Before I called the helpline I wanted to do something positive. The local garden centre had primroses and marigolds on offer, row upon row of glorious colour. I bought thirty and created a little border near the back door. I had accomplished something and it made me smile. A robin followed my trail, picking up the worms I'd disturbed. It was as if nature was trying to tell me that I was going to be OK.

I then spoke to a very nice lady on the helpline who took me through two questionnaires to grade my symptoms of depression and anxiety, and scored highly in both. She told me that I needed urgent counselling but she wasn't qualified to arrange it. I had to speak to someone else but the waiting list to speak to that person was several weeks. Not only that, but the waiting list for counselling once I'd been accepted was a minimum of nine months. I couldn't believe it. If I'd been diagnosed with breast cancer, I would be treated within a month, but it seemed to me that because I 'only' had mental health issues that it could be almost a year before I got professional help. I asked her if it would be easier to get counselling if I did harm myself. She nervously laughed and told me not to. I then asked her what would stop me while I waited nine months for help, and she had no answers. All she could do was apologise for how the system worked. It dawned on me that this was the norm for most people with mental health issues in the UK and I was embarrassed that I hadn't known the differences in the ways physical and mental health were assessed and treated.

I dutifully booked the second call in a month's time and then went back to bed for the rest of the day. I was going to have to get better by myself. I had one month of sick leave to rebuild myself and no idea where to start. How do you fix something that's broken when you don't know what needs repairing?

It was a struggle getting out of bed for the first few days. I was overwhelmed by apathy. Just getting in the shower took an almighty effort. When Dermot came home from work I felt so guilty that I hadn't sorted out what to eat at night or loaded the washing machine. He told me to stop worrying and that he would take care of everything.

I started to think about what the GP had said. What was I passionate about? The pressure of having to find the one thing that would fulfil me was exhausting. Dermot was worried that I'd spend the whole month inside alone and wanted me to try to meet new people. I scoured the internet looking for local courses but the only things that interested me were solitary activities. I didn't want to meet new people until I'd come to terms with what had happened.

Instead, I tried to focus on the little things I could do. Baby steps. I told Dermot I was going to smile at someone every day. It got me out of the house and also meant I would have to make eye contact with a stranger. That was completely outside of my comfort zone as I normally kept my head down looking at my phone or the pavement as I walked. I kept my promise and did it every day but I felt so guilty for smiling when I was meant to be on sick leave. What if someone saw me enjoying myself and it got back to my colleagues?

Chester loved having me at home. He was used to being in the garden during the day but now he had my constant attention. I sat on the kitchen floor for hours with his head in my lap. It was almost as if he could sense I wasn't happy and this was his way of giving me a hug.

After a couple of weeks the citalopram started to kick in. I still didn't have a thing to be passionate about and I hadn't made any new friends but I felt a little less fragile. I remembered I had a triathlon to train for and forced myself to go out for a bike ride. I turned to books to try to understand what was happening to me. Jenny recommended *Depressive Illness: The Curse of the Strong* by Dr Tim Cantopher and it was a revelation. He described exactly how I was feeling and it was reassuring to know that I wasn't alone. I reached out to a couple of women

I knew through social media and they helped bring me out of the darkness. The first was Alys Cole-King, a psychiatrist and director of a mental health training organisation. She listened and shared her hope that I could get through tough times. She told me about https://StayingSafe.net, a website that I could use if I ever felt suicidal. I made a Safety Plan and drew up a list of people to call if I ever started to struggle again. The second was an NHS chief executive who'd written about her own experiences of depression. She was so caring and supportive. I was lucky to be able to share what I was going through with someone who had been there and understood what it was like. She also gave me hope that I would eventually get better.

All too soon the month was up and I had to go back to work. I spent the night tossing and turning as the nightmares came back. My palms were sweating as I gripped the steering wheel, trying to focus on just driving to the hospital instead of some of the impulses running through my brain and thinking life wasn't worth living. It was only when I got out of the car and started walking towards the hospital that I realised how unprepared I was. I hadn't thought about how to explain my absence. I was worried that I'd be thrown in the deep end with an operating list the next day on patients I hadn't met.

In the end it wasn't as bad as I'd thought. I headed down to clinic, where I was welcomed with open arms. I actually felt happy when I went up to the office at lunchtime and texted Dermot on the way to tell him that I'd survived my first clinic. There was a large brown envelope on my desk. Intrigued, I opened it and my world fell apart. It was a complaint from a patient I'd operated on previously who'd unfortunately developed a late complication in my absence. Because I had done the initial operation, I was expected to deal with the complaint.

I wondered what had happened to the rest of my patients while I'd been off sick. The only way I could get through the afternoon clinic was to put the mask back on.

I had an appointment with Occupational Health the following week. I'd been putting it off as I didn't want to have depression on my record and was terrified of the consequences. Simon, the consultant, explained that everything I told him was confidential and he couldn't share it with anyone unless I gave my consent. Relieved that I could finally be honest with someone, I told him the truth. He was so kind and compassionate as I sat there crying in front of him. He said that the Trust would pay for me to see a psychologist within a few weeks. He then asked, 'Why did you only have one month off work?'

'I thought that's all I was entitled to.'

'But you could have had six months on full pay followed by six months on half pay.'

I wish I'd known. I would never have come back to work so soon, but it was too late now. Two weeks later I had an appointment to see the psychologist. I went into her office and she told me to sit down. There were two comfy armchairs facing each other.

'Which one do I sit in?'

'It doesn't matter.'

I was paralysed by indecision. Was this a test? Did it matter which chair I chose? I picked the one facing the door, clutching my coat in my lap like a comfort blanket as she asked me what had been going on. Together we started picking through the mess that had got me to her door. It was harrowing. I cried and cried. I didn't realise how much I'd been bottling things up and how far away I was from truly being well again.

I was desperate to learn how to cope at work but she wanted to focus on my health. I needed to look after myself physically before I could tackle bigger problems. She gave me strategies to help me sleep better and eat properly and told me to start having fun with Dermot again. I continued to see her every couple of weeks and as I followed her advice to the letter, work became easier as a consequence. I felt almost positive after our final session.

Triathlon training was a huge help. Whether I was swimming laps, plodding around the local fields or getting the miles in on my bike, I forgot about everything for a while. I bought a wetsuit and booked my first open-water swim session. It was freezing. I was meant to swim to a marker in the distance but without my glasses I was blind as a bat. I didn't care. There was something so peaceful about swimming in a lake, listening to the birds without having to turn all the time.

Race day arrived and I lined up with the thousands of other competitors to rack my bike before squeezing into my wetsuit. Dermot gave me a huge hug and sent me off to hear the race briefing. We entered in packs of fifty, treading water until it was time to go. Once the kicking and splashing had stopped as the faster swimmers set off, I found a gentle rhythm and forty minutes later I'd finished the mile. I peeled off my wetsuit, put on my helmet and pushed my bike to the start line, ready to ride forty kilometres in wet Lycra. It was great to hear Dermot cheering me on as I cycled past. All that was left was the ten-kilometre run. It was humbling to see so many people of all shapes and sizes running for charity. I made a point of cheering everyone who had their name written on their vest, and the crowds were amazing. It was a three-lap course and as I completed the first, I heard someone shout my name. It was my parents! Dermot had arranged for them to come and see me as a surprise. I was crying as I crossed the finish line, struggling to believe that I'd managed to complete it despite everything I'd been through. I had the bug and immediately signed up to do a longer-distance triathlon the following year.

A few weeks later, the hospital legal team contacted me about the complaint. The patient was now suing the Trust, which meant I could end up in court defending my actions and I had to draft a formal witness statement. Although she wasn't suing me, I did take it personally. I started to doubt my surgical skills again. The number of operations I felt confident to perform got smaller and smaller like an ever-decreasing circle. I wanted to stick to the simple, straightforward procedures I'd done hundreds of times before instead of the more challenging reconstructive cases. My mood darkened and I thought of ending my life once more.

One morning in November, I was called down to oncology to see a patient. She was a member of staff who'd been having chemotherapy to shrink her cancer but the tumour had stopped responding. The oncologist wanted her to have surgery in the next couple of weeks and continue with chemo afterwards. She needed an implant reconstruction and wanted me to be her surgeon. I went into autopilot and dutifully measured her up but inside I was shaking. It would be my first reconstruction since the complaint. The stakes were huge.

The day before her surgery, I was eating lunch in my car as usual, but my hands wouldn't stop shaking. I simply couldn't live like this anymore. I hunkered down in my seat trying to hide from the frustrated drivers looking for a parking space. It was time to plan how I was going to end my life. I felt sick at the thought of it. I was terrified of actually doing it, but I was too scared to keep on living. As I ran through options in my head, desperately trying to decide what to do, once and for all, I kept getting interrupted by thoughts about what the people who love me would say. They'd tell me that my life is worth living. There is always hope. They would do anything to help me get through the pain I was in. But they weren't in my shoes. They would never understand.

I had the afternoon off. It had to be now. I couldn't wait any longer. But as I turned the key in the ignition, ready to drive home, I suddenly visualised how Dermot would feel when he came home and saw what I had done. My hand fell away to my lap as tears ran down my face. I couldn't do it to him. Not without saying good-bye. I wasn't ready to die. Not yet. A tiny part of me was still clinging on to the hope of a happier future. I remembered my safety plan. I took another deep breath and slowly got out of the car. I found myself outside the medical director's office. By some miracle she was free and saw me straight away.

'I need help,' I said. 'I can't work anymore.'

'What's wrong?'

I couldn't bring myself to tell her the truth. I lied and said I was overwhelmed with stress again. The fear of admitting I was suicidal and the potential damage that would do to my career wasn't a risk I was willing to take. I told her I was meant to be operating on a member of staff the next day but I wasn't safe to do it. The guilt I felt about letting my patient down was huge. She'd specifically chosen me to be her surgeon. Not only was she dealing with the mental anguish of losing a breast, but if I didn't turn up tomorrow, she would have to deal with a different surgeon greeting her on the ward in the morning.

The medical director told me to go home and said she'd handle everything. I promised to talk to Occupational Health and my GP and not come back until they both thought I was ready. I personally didn't think I would ever be ready when work was the root of the problem. But that was for the future. All I needed to do was get home.

I should have felt a sense of relief as I walked back to my car. I was officially on sick leave. I didn't need to go in to work tomorrow. Instead, I felt numb. Fear started to creep in. The reality of what had almost happened. A second close call and I hadn't seen the warning signs. How on earth did I explain this to Dermot and my parents for the second time? None of them had a clue about how unwell I'd become. I was an expert at masking my true feelings from everyone, including myself. They all thought I was better. I guess I was more broken than I'd thought. Depression had been slowly creeping up on me, so slowly that I hadn't noticed until it was almost too late.

I told Dermot everything when he came home from work. It broke my heart to make him cry again.

'So, what happens now?' he asked.

'I've spoken to Occupational Health. He's arranged for me to see the counsellor next week and wants me to take the rest of my paid sick leave, so that's five months at home. I've got until April to sort myself out.'

I felt so guilty when I saw the psychologist again. In the last six months I'd gone backwards not forwards. She was brilliant. She kept reminding me that none of this was my fault. I was sick, that was all. But the treatment would take a long time, perhaps a lifetime.

She helped me see that the mask had to go. I'd become so used to wearing it that I never took it off. I'd been hiding my true feelings from the people who loved me. I had to learn to let them in. To stop being so independent. Let Dermot have the pleasure of helping me for a change. Remember that I deserved to be looked after and cared for.

Mum spent hours thinking of things I could do at home to distract myself. One morning, she suggested that I make a quilt. I dug out the sewing machine she'd bought me for my thirtieth birthday. I knocked one up in a week and was so pleased with myself. She then suggested sewing my next quilt by hand. I would still be a surgeon of sorts but operating on fabric instead of people. We found a pattern online and I spent hours painstakingly cutting out thousands of hexagons of paper and material. Having set my sights on a king-sized quilt, it was going to take me years to finish. I could pick it up whenever I was in the mood, without an urgent deadline to worry about.

In January I found another breast lump, this time on the right. I went back to see Amanda, who confirmed it was another cyst. A few weeks later, we got a cocker spaniel puppy called Hunter. Chester was getting older and we thought it might give him a new lease of life. It was adorable to see them snuggle up together on Chester's huge bed. I loved taking Hunter to puppy training and it was nice to have something new that Dermot and I could do together.

I started baking again and Dermot sent me on a sourdough course in London. I came away with a bubbling starter and three loaves of bread. I also discovered that eating half a kilo of fresh bread and butter in one afternoon was a great way to recover after a hard session on the bike. I continued with my triathlon training and tried not to focus on the numbers. I had always been so competitive with myself and would think a ride had been ruined if I wasn't fast enough. My psychologist wanted me to forget about the data and just swim, cycle or run because I wanted to. Because I enjoyed it. Not because a training plan told me I had to. I found that hard. I needed the data to tell me how well I was doing and my coach needed it to help plan my next sessions. In the end, I reached a compromise. I would still record each session but I wouldn't look at my computer until I got home. It made such a difference. Instead of beating myself up at how slow I thought I was riding, I started hearing the birds in the trees as I cycled past. It was now all about the lambs in the fields and the bluebells in the woods.

Eventually, I did have to start thinking about going back to work. There was no hope of another job being advertised close to home and I would be a terrible applicant, having spent so much time on sick leave. Dermot and I had talked about retraining in another surgical speciality, but that would mean doing on-call again and it wasn't something I was prepared to do. I had to go back. I had to look after my patients. Despite everything that had happened, I still loved breast surgery.

The psychologist had given me strict orders to start sharing my life with my colleagues and give them the chance to get to know the real me. I was a nervous wreck on the first day back. I couldn't stop imagining what they must be thinking about me, the new consultant who'd couldn't cope with the job, who everyone was having to cover for. The breast care nurses treated me with kid gloves for the first few weeks and Sally protected me from seeing the more emotional cases. She was a constant shoulder to cry on, and I don't know how I'd have coped without her.

The complaint was still hanging over me and I had several meetings with the hospital lawyer as the court date got closer. The only thing that made me smile at work was seeing my patients after I'd operated on them. I loved watching their faces light up when they saw how neat the scar was or heard that their cancer hadn't spread.

———

In June, Dermot and I went on a cycling camp to Italy. I needed to get some climbing practice in for the triathlon later that year, and what better place than the Alps. It was physically exhausting but the views were breathtaking. On the final day of the camp, we had all been entered into a sportive to climb the Stelvio, one of the highest mountain passes in Europe. It's twenty-one kilometres long with forty-eight hairpin bends. I stopped at every one to take a selfie and catch my breath, marvelling at the scenery around me. It got harder to breathe the higher I went and the snow on the side of the road was almost as tall as I was as I climbed the final kilometre. After one huge effort to cross the finish line, I broke out into an enormous smile. I'd climbed my first mountain. Now all I had to do was ride back to where I'd started. I was a little apprehensive, but because the roads were closed I could relax and take my time without the fear of being hit by a motorbike coming the other way. Cycling down that mountain was the most fun I have ever had on a bike. I learned to throw my weight as I went round the corners at speed, hitting over sixty kilometres an hour at times. This is why people ride up mountains – so they can fly down them afterwards.

One week later, I noticed a breast lump in the mirror. This time it was on the left, just on the edge of my cleavage. I hadn't noticed it before. Lifting my left arm, I closed my eyes so I could concentrate on what my right hand was feeling. The surgeon in me took over. Left breast, upper inner quadrant, nine o'clock, two by two centimetres, round, firm. No nodes. Probably a cyst. I made a mental note to check it in a couple of weeks. My parents had just moved to Scotland and I was chatting to my mum on the phone. I wasn't going to mention it but something made me bring it up.

'Why haven't you had it checked out?'

'It's just a cyst, Mum. I only had a mammogram nine months ago.'

'I know, but still. I worry about you.'

I told her I'd make an appointment with my GP once I got off the phone. Two weeks later I was back in Amanda's clinic again. One of the breast care nurses recognised me as she walked past. 'What are you doing here?' she asked.

'Just another cyst. You know how it is.'

And then I was called through.

Chapter 20

'Back again?' said Amanda.

'You know me. I can't stay away.'

'OK, let's have a look.'

I got undressed behind the curtain and she came through to examine me.

'How long has it been there?'

'About a month now. What do you think?' I asked.

'I'm not sure. Your breasts are very lumpy. It's not as smooth as a cyst but it's not typical for a cancer.'

'That's what I thought.'

'OK. Let's get you scanned.'

After a normal mammogram, I went through to have an ultrasound. The radiologist squeezed a dollop of cold jelly on my cleavage and placed the probe on my breast. I turned to look at the screen. I was expecting to see a well-defined circle with a dark centre. Instead, I saw a large lesion with an irregular outline and a fuzzy grey centre, about three centimetres in size. It was an obvious cancer. In that split second a light went out in my head. I knew I'd need chemotherapy. I knew I'd need a mastectomy. I knew the answers to questions I shouldn't even be thinking about. I couldn't process it all. It couldn't be happening.

I saw the radiologist's face change. Amanda came in, took one look at the screen and squeezed my hand. All three of us knew what we were dealing with.

'Do you want me to call Dermot while we do the biopsy?'

'Yes please. He'll be in theatre four.'

I hadn't asked him to come with me because I was sure it was nothing serious. The radiologist scanned my armpit and reassured me that the lymph nodes looked normal.

Then she drew up the local anaesthetic. I've told hundreds of women over the years that it might feel like a nettle sting before I did a biopsy and now I was about to find out if I'd been telling the truth.

'Sharp scratch.'

I didn't feel the needle going in but I felt a warm burning sensation as the drug started to work. She made a tiny nick in my skin with a scalpel before pushing the biopsy gun into my breast, and fired it three times. I was used to warning my patients about the loud noise the gun made but it still made me jump.

Dermot had managed to find someone to cover his list and a nurse called us back into Amanda's room. She'd arranged for me to have an urgent MRI because the cancer hadn't shown up on the mammogram.

'I'll see if I can pull some strings and get a provisional result for Friday.'

'OK.'

'One last thing. Think about who you want to treat you because I'm not sure I can.'

Dermot looked confused but I knew what she meant. It was hard to operate on people you knew. Emotionally, the stakes were much higher. And Amanda wasn't just an old boss. She'd become a good friend as well. As we walked back to the car, I could see that Dermot was struggling to keep it together.

'It might not be cancer,' he said.

I took his hand and stayed quiet. I'd seen lots of husbands in denial over the years. I wanted to let Dermot believe what he needed to so we could get through what lay ahead.

The next two days at work were a blur. I couldn't justify calling in sick when there wasn't anything officially wrong with me yet. I found a breast cancer in a woman in her thirties and had an awful flashback as I did the biopsy. Once she'd left the room, Sally asked me if I was OK.

'Yes thanks. It's just that she's so young, that's all.'

I didn't want anyone to know what I was going through. I managed to keep up the pretence that everything was fine during my afternoon operating list but it was a real struggle. I was grateful that there were only a couple of simple cases.

The MRI department fitted me in the following evening, and I didn't want to go. I'd heard patients talk about how noisy and claustrophobic it could be and I wasn't looking forward to experiencing it myself. After I'd changed into a gown, one of the radiologists asked me to lift it at the front before sticking cod-liver oil capsules on my nipples with surgical tape.

'Free health supplements?' I laughed.

'It's an anatomy marker for the doctor reading the scan. Sometimes the nipples don't show up.'

I lay on my front with my breasts hanging down and the radiologist pushed earplugs into my ears before covering them with a pair of headphones. I spent the next forty minutes listening to the grinding and clunking of the machine as the scans were taken.

At home, I was a wreck. I couldn't sleep. In the middle of the night I scoured the internet for more information even though I knew what was going to happen. I used to tell my patients to stay off the internet, but I couldn't stop scrolling. I ordered book after book written by other cancer patients, hoping they would guide me through treatment. When Dermot got home from work on Thursday I persuaded him to drive us to the coast. It was a balmy summer's evening and I wanted to create a happy memory before our lives got turned upside down. We splashed in the sea with the dogs, laughing at them chasing balls in the sand. I tried to cling on to the feeling of my hair blowing in the wind, knowing it would be gone in a couple of weeks.

Dermot met me in the breast unit the next morning and we sat next to the other couples anxiously waiting for results. You could cut the tension with a knife. I watched a mum and daughter walk past us in tears, and Dermot gave my hand an extra squeeze.

Lisa, one of the breast care nurses, called us through and Amanda got straight to the point.

'It's cancer.'

She then started crying. Dermot was crying. Lisa was crying. The only one not crying was me. I felt like I was floating, looking down on everything happening below. Even though I'd known what was coming, it still didn't make it real.

'I don't have the receptors or the MRI results yet,' she said, 'but I've talked to Dr Moody. She wants to give you chemo first to try and shrink it down.'

Dermot held my hand even tighter than before.

Lisa then asked me if I wanted to use a false name so members of staff who knew me wouldn't know I had cancer. The first thing that came to mind was to use my porn star name – my first pet and my mum's maiden name. Mine is Max Love. I couldn't imagine a nurse calling that out in a waiting room and I wasn't sure I'd remember it once chemotherapy took hold. I was also bound to be recognised as I walked around the hospital between scans and appointments. I didn't want it to be a secret. I wasn't ashamed of having cancer and had nothing to hide.

'No thanks. I'll stay as Liz.'

Amanda arranged to see me the following Wednesday with the rest of the results and then I'd see Dr Moody in the afternoon. I bit my lip as I walked out of her room. Dermot took me out through a side door and we crumpled on to a bench, sobbing. It was so unfair. How on earth could I get breast cancer after everything I'd been through? As we sat in the car on the way home, I kept running through the worst-case scenarios. The risk of recurrence. The risk of death. I didn't need to Google anything. It was all in my head.

The first thing I had to do was call my parents. Mum was in the garden planting flowers.

'Is Dad with you?'

'No. He's upstairs.'

'Go and get him, then sit on the sofa.'

I told them what no parent wants to hear. I went through the treatment I was going to have and how long it would take.

'It must be bad if you need chemotherapy,' said Mum.

'Not necessarily. It's often used to shrink cancers so women can avoid a mastectomy.'

'You sound like you're talking about a patient instead of yourself.'

'I'm just trying to hold it together. I know too much.'

I couldn't share with them the horror story in my head. I knew what my future might hold; they didn't. I wanted to protect them. The worst part was when I said goodbye. What I really, really needed was a great big hug from my mum but she was hundreds of miles away in Scotland. At least she had Dad for support.

After calling my colleagues to let them know I wouldn't be coming in for a while, Dermot and I worked our way through our phone book as we told our closest friends. There was a lot of crying followed by a lot of swearing. We were both a bit broken by the time we'd finished. We went up to bed but neither of us slept. Dermot curled around me, holding me tight in his arms. I could feel him shudder as he cried. I turned to face him and gave him a kiss.

'I'm sorry.'

'What for?' he said.

'For getting depression. For getting cancer. You didn't sign up for this when you married me.'

'Don't be daft. I love you. Nothing changes that. We'll get through this together.'

The next day the alarm went off at five in the morning. Back in the spring we'd signed up to do our cycling club's annual ride to the coast for breakfast and I was determined to do it. As I chatted away to the cyclists around me, I forgot all about cancer and chemotherapy. I was just Liz. The bacon sandwich was one of the best I've ever had and it more than made up for the rain and wind. As I got closer to home, I couldn't get my head around the fact that I would be having chemotherapy in a week. I'd just cycled one hundred miles. I'd ridden up the Stelvio the month before. I was the fittest I'd ever been. I had no symptoms. None of it made sense.

Amanda now had all of my results. It was a mixture of oestrogen-sensitive ductal and lobular cancer. The MRI had shown that it was almost six centimetres in size. Lobular cancers can be sneaky and often impossible to see on mammograms and ultrasounds, but even I was surprised at how large it was. How had I not noticed it before?

Amanda asked me where I wanted to have surgery. I'd wrestled long and hard about this decision. I knew every breast surgeon in the UK by name or reputation. I could take my pick. Despite that, I wanted to stay with her. She'd trained me, I trusted her completely and it was close to home if there were any complications.

'I want to stay here with you.'

'OK, but I can only do this if we stop being friends until you've finished treatment. From now on, I have to treat you like a patient. No more coffee and cake.'

'I know. I'll miss you, though.'

'Me too.'

There was an hour to kill before meeting Dr Moody. Dermot had some work to do but he'd arranged for me to speak to a nurse called Julie. She'd had chemotherapy the year before and had offered to chat. She was exactly what I needed at that moment in time. She told me what to expect and how to cope and promised to come and sit with me during my first infusion. Seeing her back at work so soon after treatment gave me hope that I could do the same. I then went to buy a magazine to read and bumped into Amanda at the till. I turned to say 'Hi' and she nodded back. No more gossiping like we used to.

I rushed out to the car and started crying; not because of cancer but because of how my life was already changing. I heard a knock on the window and looked up to see Dermot. He must have had a sixth sense about how I was feeling. He gave me a hug and said, 'Everything's going to be all right.'

As we sat in the oncology waiting room I suddenly realised how serious this all was. I was surrounded by other cancer patients and they all looked sick. That was how I would look in a few months' time. Dr Moody said she was going to give me six three-weekly cycles of chemotherapy, starting with docetaxel and then switching to a combination of three drugs called FEC.

'I need to go through the side effects and complications of the drugs.'

'Assume I don't know anything. It will make it easier for both of us,' I said.

'OK. Let's start with your hair. It's going to fall out unless you try a cold cap. Have you any thoughts?'

This was one thing I had read about. The cold cap would give me an ice-cream headache as it cooled down my scalp to try to prevent the chemo drugs from reaching my hair follicles. I'd have to wear it for a couple of hours before each infusion to give it a chance to work and for an hour or so afterwards. I wanted to spend as little time as possible on the unit and I actually wasn't that bothered about losing my hair. I was curious to see what I'd look like bald.

'I don't want to use it,' I said.

'OK. Next. Do you have children?'

Dermot and I were still deciding whether we wanted a child of our own. He already had a grown-up daughter from his first marriage. After spending the first year of our marriage living apart, I'd wanted a year of just the two of us before children came along. Getting depressed had thrown a spanner in the works.

'Not yet,' I said.

'Well, your cancer is large. You're forty and the treatment will probably make you infertile. If you did want to try egg preservation first, the hormones could speed up how quickly the cancer is growing. There's a chance it will spread before you start chemotherapy. I'm not sure it's wise to take that risk.'

Dermot and I looked at each other. In less than a minute my fertility had been taken away from me. I swallowed back my tears.

'No egg preservation.'

'Next. Sepsis. Chemo attacks the bone marrow, which

means a simple infection can kill. You need to check your temperature every day and if it goes above thirty-eight degrees, you must come straight to the hospital.'

She handed me a card with the emergency contact number and then went through the rest of the side effects.

'One last decision. How do you want to have the drugs? Through a PICC line or a port?'

A PICC line is a long tube inserted in the upper arm. It is covered in a dressing to stop it getting infected. I didn't want to risk Hunter jumping up and pulling it out so I asked for a port. This would be inserted just beneath my collarbone and the chemo nurses accessed it by sticking a needle through the skin into the chamber below. The only problem was that I wanted to start chemo in two days' time but there was no space on the anaesthetist's list. One of Dermot's colleagues found out and he offered to come in on his day off to do it. I was overwhelmed by his kindness and hoped one day I'd be able to return the favour.

When we got home, Dermot and I went through our diaries and started cancelling everything we'd arranged between now and Christmas. It was so hard unpicking all our plans. Instead of holidays and concerts to look forward to, we now faced five months of misery and pain. Dermot didn't deserve this.

I had one more day before chemotherapy and I had no idea what to do with myself. I'd already packed a bag of things to take with me based on Julie's advice. Mum and Dad were arriving that night to look after me during the day while Dermot was at work. I was still trying to figure out what to say if someone recognised me coming out of the oncology unit. Dermot suggested I start writing a blog. I loved the idea. I didn't want to hide the fact that I had cancer, and it would be a good way to update family and friends about what I was going through. He was in his element as he set up a website for me, and I started jotting down what had happened over the last couple of weeks. I wanted to be honest and upfront, but I didn't want to scare anyone who might need treatment in the future. After getting Dermot to check what I'd written, I uploaded it to the site and sent it to everyone I knew. As their replies of sorrow and support filtered through, it gave me a boost to know that all these people had my back.

Mum had managed to find the sick blanket I used when I was a little girl for those days when I was too poorly to go to school but not too poorly to watch cartoons. She'd also bought me a small cuddly panda to take with me to every appointment when they couldn't be there in person. Mum gave me one last hug before going to bed and said, 'I wish I could have the chemotherapy for you. I'd do anything to stop you having to go through this.'

'I know, Mum. None of this is fair. But look on the bright side. It will all be over in five months and then we can celebrate properly at Christmas.'

Chapter 21

I wanted to make chemotherapy look as easy as possible so my future patients would know that it wasn't as bad as they thought, but I was scared. What if it was that bad? I didn't know how sick I would get and hated the idea of not being in control. With a slick of red lipstick for courage, I walked on to the chemo suite with Dermot by my side.

The unit was light, bright and sunny. Every patient had a huge reclining leather chair to curl up in. I was the youngest patient in the room by a good thirty years and felt very sorry for myself. Once I was hooked up to the infusion, Dermot got out the cribbage board. He'd taught me to play when we got engaged and I was convinced he was making up the rules when he shouted 'one for his nob'. We'd only played a few hands when Julie arrived, letting Dermot escape to clear his head. She'd brought me a cup of tea and a bag of bits and pieces that had helped her cope with chemo. We chatted for the best part of an hour until Dermot came back to carry on with the game. I was sure he was missing points when he scored my hand and loudly declared that he was cheating. The nurses were on my side and started joining in. By the time he let me win, the infusion was over. I was sent home with a big green party bag full of drugs to cope with the side effects: steroids, laxatives, antacids, anti-sickness pills, antibiotics, antifungals and bone-marrow-boosting injections that I had to give myself every day for a week.

My nose started to twitch in the car on the way home and I had a metallic taste in my mouth, but that was all. I went into the kitchen and it looked like a florist had exploded. Mum had been busy arranging bunches of flowers sent by family and friends and there was a huge pile of cards to open. Dermot made us all a cup of tea and I spat it out. It was revolting. If I'd realised that the cup I'd had with breakfast would be the last one I'd enjoy for a while, I'd have had about three.

By the evening things had started to happen. I was cold and shivery; my mouth was sore and I felt very sick. My tongue was covered in a slimy white coating and even water tasted disgusting. Over the next twenty-four hours the fatigue started to kick in, like a hangover from hell. I felt like I'd been hit with a chemical sledgehammer. Everything ached, from my teeth to my toes. I became incredibly constipated, which gave me colicky abdominal pain. My lips started to crack, my nose started to bleed and the weight was falling off me. Finally, I lost the ability to think. I'd read about chemo-brain and now I was experiencing it. I couldn't concentrate on anything and spent hours staring into space. One evening we were sitting on the sofa and I asked Dermot to pass me the TV remote.

'What?'

'The remote,' I said. 'It's on the table but I can't reach it.'

'I don't know what you mean.'

'The remote. The thing you turn the telly on with.'

He started to laugh. I'd actually been asking for a potato. I'd got the words muddled up in my head and hadn't realised.

Eventually Mum and Dad had to go home, leaving Dermot to look after me. I felt so sorry for him. I was surrounded by flowers and cards but he needed support as well. I couldn't imagine how hard it was going to be for him to go to work and leave me on my sick bed. Later that night, I asked, 'What's it like to see me go through this?'

'I feel impotent,' he said. 'I'm a doctor and I can't do anything to make you better.'

That only made me feel worse. I dragged myself off the sofa to give him a hug.

'I couldn't get through this without you.'

Several women had messaged me through my blog to tell me how to cope and the one piece of advice they'd all given was to keep active. One of my neighbours, Ellen, offered to walk with me and we met at half-six every morning for a gentle stroll around the village. It was wonderful to get some fresh air and talk about anything but cancer for a while. I also felt less guilty about spending the rest of the day on the sofa, lost in my own thoughts. As the days went by I struggled to cope – and I was young and fit with Dermot to look after me. I couldn't believe how easily I'd recommended chemotherapy in meetings. Would I ever be able to tell a patient she needed it now that I knew what it was really like?

I asked Julie when my hair would start to fall out. She said that her pubic hair fell out on day ten and the rest happened a few days later. I was shocked. I had no idea that chemo patients lost all their hair. Free Brazilian and leg wax on the NHS. Who knew? Dermot went to make an appointment to get my head shaved at the end of the following week. When he came home, he told me that he'd started to cry in the hairdressers. I felt awful. This was all my fault.

By the time the weekend came around, I'd turned a corner. Dermot suggested that we went for a low-key bike ride and as we gently pedalled down country lanes I felt a flicker of hope. For that one hour I forgot what was happening to me and what was yet to come. I came down to earth with a bang, though, when my hands became stiff and my fingertips began to peel. My nails were so sore that I couldn't open a can of Coke or do up a button and I began to lose sensation as my fingers became calloused. It was a struggle getting dressed and I now had to use both hands to drink in case I dropped my glass on the floor. There was a risk that the numbness could be permanent and this was a real worry. Without functioning fingers, I might never operate again.

As Julie had predicted, my pubic hair fell out on day ten. Three days later, as I gathered my hair into a ponytail, strands started to come away in my hands. Every time I touched my head, more came out. I didn't think I could wait another few days for the shave. The hairdressers agreed to squeeze me in the following evening so Dermot could take me after work. As I washed my hair for the last time I couldn't stop crying. I hadn't realised how much this would affect me. Would Dermot still find me attractive? I didn't know how to tell him what I was feeling yet I was desperate to know what he thought.

My hairdresser already had tears in her eyes as I sat down. She started at the back so I couldn't see what was happening, but the moment she reached the front, I gulped. I didn't like what I saw. I could see in the mirror that Dermot was trying not to cry, so I plastered a smile on my face to be strong for both of us. They wouldn't let us pay and that did make me cry.

The first thing I did when I got home was to make myself look in the mirror. My hand automatically went up to my face to tuck my hair behind my ears, but there was nothing there. I didn't recognise the person staring back at me. I no longer felt like a woman. How much worse would it be when I lost my breast as well?

I felt so vulnerable as I lay in bed next to Dermot. He curled around me to give me a cuddle but I flinched when he touched my scalp. I wrapped my arms tightly around my chest so he wouldn't feel the cancer. I hated pushing him away but I wasn't ready to let him in. Dermot was having none of it and curled even closer around me.

'It's OK,' he said. 'I'm not going anywhere.'

By the time the third week came around I almost felt normal again apart from the sore hands and mouth and the loss of taste, and then the menopause kicked in, thanks to chemo switching off my ovaries. Out of nowhere I felt a wave of heat rush up my body, flushing my face and making me sweat. I was in the middle of our village shop and I had to rush to the freezer cabinet until I cooled down. The flushes came every hour and I spent my days constantly stripping off. That evening, I woke up in the middle of the night thinking I'd wet myself as a trickle of warm liquid ran down my inner thigh. I realised this was my first night sweat, and they came every hour as well. Nights were now spent tossing the duvet covers off, searching for a cold spot on the pillow. I knew the tamoxifen I'd have to take for ten years after chemo, to stop the cancer coming back, would make me feel the same. How on earth was I going to cope?

As cycle two got nearer I felt more and more anxious. Now that I knew how bad chemo would make me feel there was no way I was going through it again. Except I had no choice. There were another five sessions left. To make the most of my final good day for a while, I decided to cycle to my next infusion. It was a glorious morning and the sun was shining brightly. Dermot had plotted out a quiet route along country lanes and I loved every minute. I felt free. I couldn't stop smiling as I sat outside waiting for him to pick up the bike. Unlike last time, he had back-to-back meetings and Julie was busy for the first hour but I wasn't worried. I'd brought a book to read and was sure the time would fly by. Except it didn't. I was the only patient without someone to keep them company. I felt so alone. I buried my head in the book, desperately trying not to cry.

I was so pleased to see Julie when she finally arrived.

'How's it going?' she asked.

'It's all a bit shit, isn't it?'

'I've brought you one of the sun hats I used to wear, to stop your head burning in the sun. Have the hot flushes started yet?'

'With a vengeance. It's like an orgasm in reverse. I can feel it coming but I definitely don't want it.'

The elderly gentleman sitting behind us burst out laughing.

I wanted to keep my fitness up during this cycle and remembered the Saturday-morning parkrun that I'd done a couple of times the year before. In the car on the way home, I asked Dermot if he'd do it with me the next day, before the symptoms kicked in. It was another hot sunny morning and I'd decided not to wear a cap to hide my bald head. Dermot stayed with me as I slowly jogged the whole five kilometres. At the finish, an older man came up to me and gave me the biggest hug.

'I'm Steven. Welcome to the cuddle club.'

He told me that he was having treatment for a metastatic sarcoma and introduced me to another couple of runners who were also having treatment. It was so nice to feel part of a community again.

The next day my symptoms were back but everything had been ramped up a notch. I was so constipated that I sent Dermot to the pharmacist for some suppositories, but they didn't work. In desperation and shame, I ended up doing a manual evacuation on myself just to get things going. I flushed my pride and dignity down the toilet as my fingers went to work.

One week later I started to feel rotten. I checked my temperature and it was normal. Dermot got me some paracetamol and we started watching a film. After an hour or so I felt worse. I was shivering on the sofa and my pulse was racing. I checked my temperature again. It was thirty-eight degrees centigrade. Dermot rang the emergency number and we were told to go to straight to A&E as there were no free beds on the oncology unit. It was ten o'clock on a Friday night on a bank holiday weekend. A&E was the last place we wanted to be.

The department was heaving. We could have told the receptionist who we were so we would get seen quickly but I didn't want to make a fuss. However, the oncology nurse had rung my details through and the receptionist was expecting us. We were taken to the one remaining empty cubicle in the Children's Area.

Minutes later, a wonderful nurse called Paolo came in to sort me out. He was competent and caring and I knew I was in safe hands. Within forty minutes I'd had antibiotics, fluids and paracetamol and my pulse was coming down. Dermot and I then spent the next two and a half hours waiting to be seen by a doctor. I was finally seen at one in the morning and he told us off for not saying who we were. My bloods were back and although my inflammatory markers were normal, he was concerned that my white cell count was high. It's normally dangerously low in septic chemotherapy patients and he couldn't work out what was going on. I was going to have to stay in overnight and was whisked off to a side room on a medical ward.

The one thing I needed was sleep and it's the one thing I didn't get. I never realised how busy an acute medical ward is at night. I had my obs taken every hour, accompanied by the incessant beeping of fluid pumps all over the ward. On top of that, one of the male patients started shouting, 'Help me! Save me! Take me home!' One of the ladies in the bay opposite would then shout, 'You're a horrid man!' He would then reply, 'Well, you're a horrid woman!' This continued all through the night.

No wonder my patients had been so grumpy when I'd pitched up bright and breezy for morning ward rounds as a trainee. I felt much better in the morning and was desperate to go home. Shortly after Dermot arrived, the consultant looking after me knocked on the door. He took one look at my bald head and started crying. I felt so sorry for the junior doctor standing next to him. Once he'd composed himself, he said, 'Look, I'm not an oncologist. Have you got any idea why your white cell count is so high?'

I was shocked that he expected me to know, as I wasn't an oncologist either. However, I'd done a bit of research on my phone before he arrived.

'I'm fairly certain it's the injections I've been giving myself to stimulate the bone marrow. You could contact the on-call oncologist to check that I'm right and see if it's safe for me to go home.'

Maybe I did have to become an expert after all.

The next two weeks were the same as before and soon I was back in the chair for the third infusion. We did the parkrun again but I was noticeably more tired and had to stop and walk several times. The lack of sleep thanks to the night sweats wasn't helping. I now felt short of breath at rest. Just walking to the toilet made me dizzy and I had to shower sitting down.

My parents drove down for my birthday and it meant the world to see them, especially on my good week. I was now used to how I looked but I could see the pain in their eyes when they saw my bald head for the first time. The following weekend I should have been doing a long-distance triathlon. However, our cycling club was running a sprint-distance event at the local leisure centre and I'd managed to get one of the last places. I'd had to promise to go slowly and stop if I felt sick as there were no first aiders on the course.

Dermot dropped me off at the start. He was on-call but hoped he could complete his ward round in time to see me finish. After twelve lengths of breaststroke, I made my way to my bike to see Dermot cheering me on. I knew the roads as they were local to us, and fifty minutes later I was ready for the run. I was determined to jog every step of the way without stopping to rest or walk. It was a two-lap course and I could hear Dermot yelling as I wobbled past. I can't describe the sense of achievement I felt when I mustered up the energy to sprint across the finish line.

I saw Dr Moody before starting the next round of drugs to get the results of my mid-point MRI. It had shown that the cancer was shrinking and she was pleased with my progress.

I'd been expecting the worst and found the good news hard to take. It was a huge anti-climax.

On my last good day before starting cycle four, I went to a breast cancer conference in London. I wanted to learn about the latest developments before I went back to clinical work in the spring. It would also be nice to catch up with colleagues I hadn't seen for a year. From the moment I arrived, I knew it was completely the wrong thing to do. I stuck out like a sore thumb with my bald head. Friends didn't know what to say to me. All they wanted to talk about was my cancer. I had been reduced to an illness. As I sat in the lecture theatre listening to lectures about new ways to treat brain metastases, it was all too much. I left at the first coffee break and cried all the way home on the train. I no longer belonged in the world I knew and loved and didn't know whether I would ever fit in again.

I dragged myself in for the fourth round of treatment, curious to see how different the side effects would be. Instead of an infusion, the FEC drugs were slowly injected one at a time into my port. It was very intimate as the nurse had to sit right in front of me but she made it feel like it was the most natural thing in the world. We chatted and gossiped the whole way through.

I noticed an immediate difference in the car on the way home. I felt incredibly sick and saliva was pooling in the floor of my mouth. It got worse as the days went on and nothing touched it. Everything now tasted chalky and it was hard to find something to eat that would cut through without making me sick. I was a lot more tired and although I still walked with Ellen and did the parkruns, I could barely move afterwards. I felt old. I felt vulnerable. I was an empty shell of the woman I once was.

It was so hard driving in for the fifth cycle. I could just about handle the side effects of chemo but the nausea had been unbearable. My oncologist gave me a different antiemetic but it barely took the edge off. The cumulative effects of chemo were starting to take their toll and I didn't bounce back as quickly. My good week was now a mediocre one. I had no energy and couldn't stand the thought of having to go through this again. To make matters worse, my eyebrows started to fall out. I tried to draw them on, but without hairs to guide me I looked more like a drag queen. As I scrubbed the make-up off, the first of my eyelashes fell out.

Friends had asked how I was going to celebrate when I left the chemo unit for the last time. They didn't understand I still had a week of hell to get through and this would be the worst of the lot. I also felt guilty that I got to finish treatment when people I knew with metastatic disease were on it for life. One of them had suggested that I was doing my own triathlon of treatment – chemotherapy, surgery and radiotherapy – and I loved her for that. It helped me mentally prepare for what still lay ahead and only then would I celebrate in style.

Before my final dose of FEC, I had to see Amanda to finalise what surgery I wanted. It was a simple enough decision. Do I have a mastectomy and go flat or have an implant reconstruction instead? I spent my working life talking patients through the same process. Most only had weeks to make a decision. I'd had the luxury of five months and was still unsure. I hadn't given my breasts much thought until now, but suddenly I was having to analyse how important they were for my sexuality, my femininity and my identity as a woman. And it was impossible to think rationally because one of them had a huge cancer inside it.

Going flat would be the simplest option. I'd be in and out on the same day and back to normal in a couple of weeks. I'd get a soft prosthetic to put in my bra before being fitted for a silicone one when my wounds were healed. Except it wasn't that simple. I had small breasts and my wardrobe was full of deep V-neck tops and dresses. If I wore a prosthesis, I'd have to wear a full-cupped bra to hold it in place that would be visible with everything I owned. I didn't want to buy a whole new wardrobe but was vanity enough of a reason to have a reconstruction?

I was lucky that Amanda was offering me one in the first place. I knew that I would need radiotherapy because the cancer was large and we both knew the damage that could do to the implant. A thick capsule could form around it contorting it into a tight ball and causing a lot of pain. She hoped that the mesh she used to secure the implant would offer some protection but there were no guarantees. If I did go flat, the skin damage from radiotherapy would mean that it wouldn't stretch to accommodate an implant at a later date. I didn't have enough fat to have a reconstruction using my own tissue so an implant was my only chance at having a breast again. I also couldn't stop wondering what my patients would think if I didn't have a reconstruction. How could I turn down the operation I'd been trained to do?

I sat topless on the couch while Amanda measured me up for implants. The surgeon in me was paying close attention to how she did it, hoping to improve my own skills when I went back to work. As a patient I felt like an object as she gently moved my breast left and right, double-checking the numbers she'd recorded. She then consented me for the operation, rattling off the long list of side effects and possible complications. I knew this speech by heart. I said the same thing to my own patients. But being on the other side made me realise just how frightening it can be. Hearing that I could be left with permanent arm swelling and chronic pain was a lot to take in. I'd been so blasé when I'd covered these in clinic but now there was a chance I would have to live with the consequences of surgery.

Dermot sat with me while I had the final round of drugs. We'd made it. I just had to grit my teeth and get through one final week. Mum and Dad had come down to help look after me as Dermot was on-call again. It was hard to see them look at me and realise just how ill I was. No parent should have to watch their child go through this.

The rest of my lower eyelashes fell out overnight and I was hanging on to the remaining few on the top lids. As I looked at my face in the mirror, I saw a sexless alien staring back at me. I honestly had no idea how I was going to get through the final five days. I was too sick to eat and couldn't walk more than ten steps without having to stop and rest. The only thing keeping me going was knowing that I would never feel that way again. But even that was false hope. If my cancer returned in the future, there was a strong chance I'd find myself back in the chemo chair.

Two weeks later I had my final check-in with Dr Moody. My cancer had completely disappeared on the final MRI. This time I was pleased to hear good news. The last five months had been worth it. I had finally finished the swim leg of my triathlon. It was now time to rest, recharge and get ready for surgery.

Chapter 22

The day had finally arrived. I was going to find out what it was like to be on the other end of the knife. I was already awake when the alarm went off and Dermot had to remind me that I wasn't allowed a cup of tea.

'What about gin?' I asked. 'That's a clear fluid.'

I started to cry when I took off my engagement ring but I didn't want to risk leaving it in the hospital room.

The nurses on the ward were wonderful. They treated me as Liz, not Liz the surgeon or Liz, Mr O'Riordan's wife. I needed that space to be able to get my head straight for what was about to happen. The anaesthetist came to see me and I had to admit that, despite being a surgeon, I was terrified of having an anaesthetic. She reassured me and went through what would happen.

'Will it be sore afterwards?'

'Yes,' she said. 'I'll put a local anaesthetic block in and make sure you're written up for morphine in case you need it.'

'One final question. Could you be careful when you pull the tape off my eyes at the end? I want to hang on to my few remaining eyelashes.'

'I promise you that no eyelashes will be harmed. We'll use gel pads instead.'

Amanda was the last person to see me and she went over the operation one more time. I was trying to be brave and failing miserably. She gave me a hug and said she'd see me soon. A porter was waiting to push me to theatre. I asked her to give me a moment so I could say goodbye to Dermot. We were both crying. I felt so sorry for him. All I had to do was go to sleep but he had to occupy himself while I was under the knife.

As I was wheeled down the corridor I saw an anaesthetist I knew on his way to theatres. I wanted to hide. I felt so exposed as I lay on the trolley, naked under my gown with my bald head on show.

'Hi,' he said. 'What are you having done?'

'I'm going to have my left breast cut off.'

Once I was safely inside the anaesthetic room I began to relax. Amanda held tightly on to my hand while the anaesthetist started the infusion. All I can remember is crying out in pain as the drugs ran up my arm and the smiling faces of the women around me started to blur.

I woke up on the ward just after lunchtime, pain-free and high as a kite on morphine. Dermot was sitting next to me and I couldn't stop telling him that I loved him. Amanda popped in to say she was happy with how things had gone. She lifted my gown to check for bleeding. My eyes followed hers and I got a shock. I knew that the breast skin would be black and blue but it was hard to see it with my own eyes. Once Dermot left, doctors, nurses and secretaries came to visit me. I was too unsettled to sleep and word must have got around because the theatre night staff came to see me as well.

Dermot arrived bright and early the next morning and gave me a gentle hug. I handed him a pile of envelopes to lick and stick. I'd written down the name of every doctor, nurse, assistant and cleaner who'd looked after me so I could make sure I gave every one of them a thank-you card. I was always thrilled when a patient sent me a card and I wanted to share that feeling.

The morphine was wearing off and it was painful to push myself out of bed. Dermot had to help me go to the toilet and get dressed. I touched my new breast and was shocked at how little sensation there was. I could feel the pressure of my fingertips but nothing else. I'd forgotten that the breast skin would be numb.

Lisa came to see me. I broke down in front of her and all the emotion I'd been bottling up came out. It was a much-needed release and she gently told me to take one step at a time. Amanda was the last person to see me before Dermot took me home. After reminding me to do my shoulder exercises every day to get my arm moving, she told me that I couldn't run or swim for a couple of months.

'One final thing,' she said. 'No lifting anything heavier than a wine glass until I see you back in clinic.'

I was stealing that phrase when I went back to work.

I had completed the bike leg of my cancer triathlon. Dermot gently ushered me out to the car. He was an excellent servant for the first few days, bringing me drinks, painkillers and food on demand. He also put up with me moaning about how sore I was and nagged me to do my physiotherapy.

I saw Amanda after five days for a wound check. I was having a lot of pain at the side of the implant and had developed cording in my armpit. Tiny lymph vessels under the skin had thrombosed, forming tight bands that ran from my scar down towards my elbow. It was more important than ever that I kept up with my exercises to try to break the cords as I needed to get both arms above my head for radiotherapy. Some of my own patients had also had cording but the breast care nurses always looked after them. I had no idea how painful and restrict-ive it could be and was embarrassed how little I knew about it.

I carried on walking every day and, once the dressings had been taken off, I couldn't wait to have a proper shower instead of a strip-wash in the sink. It had been frosty outside and I knew the hot water would warm me up. As I lathered my implant I got another shock. The skin was icy cold to touch. Without the blood from the breast tissue underneath, there was nothing to warm it up. Again, how did I not know this before?

My results appointment was on 23 December. This time I wasn't nervous. I knew that my lymph nodes looked normal on the ultrasound scan back in July and the post-chemo MRI showed the cancer had disappeared. I felt so sorry for everyone else sitting in the waiting room expect-ing bad news, happy that I would never have to go through that again.

Amanda called us in. We sat down, nervous and excited, ready to hear the good news. She told us that the chemotherapy had melted away the ductal cancer in my breast.

'However,' she said, 'there's thirteen centimetres of lobular cancer left.'

I thought she'd said millimetres. Then I looked at her face.

'What did you say?'

'There was thirteen centimetres of lobular cancer left in the breast.'

'Shit.'

The MRI had only shown a six-centimetre cancer. That must have been the ductal part. The lobular portion had been truly occult as every scan had missed it. I'd seen it before in a couple of women but it didn't happen very often.

'There's more, I'm afraid. Two of the sentinel nodes were positive.'

'Fuck. Sorry.'

'It's OK.'

She gave me a tissue. I clung to Dermot's hand for dear life as the information sank in. I would need more surgery. More intensive radiotherapy. My odds of being alive in ten years' time were now a lot worse.

All I wanted to do was to run out of the room screaming but Amanda had to consent me for another operation to remove the rest of the nodes in my armpit. When she was finished, Dermot and I found ourselves on the same bench we'd sat on five months earlier, crying our eyes out. I couldn't tell Dermot how bad the news was. I didn't want him to know. He would tell me not to worry and that it might not happen but I knew too much.

I would have to deal with that knowledge alone. Then, with a sense of déjà vu, we both had the difficult job of telling our families. I rang Mum and yet again had to tell her to go and get Dad and sit down. Doing it so close to Christmas made it worse. It wasn't real. It couldn't be real.

Chapter 23

There was nothing for it but to plaster on a smile and get through Christmas with Dermot's family. His parents' house was full of noise and laughter and it was a welcome distraction from the turmoil in my head but there were still moments when I wobbled. It was painful to watch his nieces and nephews opening their presents knowing that I would never get to see my own child do the same.

New Year's Eve was harder still. The future was bleak. There was now an even greater chance that my cancer would come back and I needed to get Dermot to acknowledge it. Ever an optimist, he wanted me to stop worrying about something that might never happen, but I couldn't let it go.

Eventually, he snapped. 'Fine. I'll say it. You might die before me. Are you happy now?'

'Yes,' I said.

'You do know I'm more likely to die first, don't you?'

'Don't say that.'

'Well, it's true. I'm ten years older than you, and your cancer might not come back.'

The next morning Dermot woke me up with a cup

of tea. 'Right. No more being miserable. You need to move on.'

I thought back to something my psychologist had suggested: to keep a gratitude journal and write down three things every day that I was thankful for. It had seemed too much like hard work at the time and I still wasn't sure I wanted the daily chore, but it had given me an idea. I rummaged around in the back of a kitchen cupboard until I found an old vase. I cut up strips of coloured paper and put them in a small glass next to it.

'I have a plan,' I said. 'Every time something good happens, we're going to write it down and put it in the vase.'

'Good idea.'

'I mean it. You're going to do it too. And it doesn't have to be every day. I'm going to call it my jar of joy.'

We spent the rest of the day in the garden. Dermot went to shower while I got supper ready. He came into the kitchen smiling and reached for a strip of paper.

'You're filling one in? I never thought you'd actually do it. What's it for?'

'I haven't worn these trousers in months and I found a five-pound note in the pocket.'

'Remind me to check your pockets in the future.'

Later that evening, while we were watching TV, Dermot handed me a strip of paper and a pen.

'Your turn?'

'What for?' I asked.

'Your first note for the jar.'

He called the dogs through from the kitchen and while Chester rested his head on a cushion, Dermot lifted Hunter on to my lap.

'I know we've never allowed the dogs in the lounge but I think it's about time you got to cuddle Hunter on the sofa.'

That was definitely something to smile about.

One week later I was back on the ward to have my axillary lymph nodes removed. I could see the sadness in the nurses' eyes. They knew that my cancer had spread to my armpit because of the operation I was having. My brave face was long gone. I kept my eyes shut as I was taken to theatre. I knew I'd start crying if anyone talked to me. Amanda held my hand and the anaesthetist placed the oxygen mask over my nose and mouth. She told me to breathe normally but I started to panic. I was scared of what Amanda would find when she went back inside. Comforting words started to fade as the drugs went to work.

I woke up on the ward feeling a bit sorry for myself. Dermot came to see me later that afternoon with a cheeky grin on his face. He took out his phone and showed me a video. I saw myself in recovery declaring undying love for him as I quoted lyrics from a nineties love song. I watched myself giggling while trying to be serious like the world's happiest drunk. If I hadn't seen the video, I would have sworn that it hadn't happened.

Once Dermot went home I spent a sleepless night on morphine. I had another stream of visitors but this time it was different. Several nurses I'd worked with in the past came to sit with me and share their own cancer stories. For some of them it was the first time they'd told anyone outside their family and I felt honoured that I could help them in some small way. It was hard hearing how they had struggled to look after cancer patients while dealing with their own illness and I started to wonder what it would be like for me.

The two weeks waiting for results was much harder this time around. I spent a lot of dark hours in the middle of the night playing around with online scoring systems. I wanted to know how bad my prognosis would be if all the lymph nodes were involved. Dermot kept telling me to stop, but I couldn't. I'd never seen a patient with a tumour as large as mine and got a kind of sick pleasure in speculating about my fate.

The cording in my arm was getting worse and seriously restricted my shoulder movement. I also developed a new pain on my chest wall, like a burning electric shock. I knew it was a consequence of the nerves in the skin being divided when the breast was removed and had always told my own patients that it might happen. Now I was finding out for myself just how painful it could be. Then we had to have Chester put to sleep. Dermot and I were in pieces as we took him to the vets. Even Hunter seemed lost at home without his furry friend to snuggle up with.

I had grown to hate the breast clinic waiting room. I kept my eyes focused on the floor as I rocked back and forth in the chair. Dermot reached for my hand but it didn't help. Lisa called us in and I could see that Amanda was smiling.

'It's good news. Only one of the eight nodes was involved,' she said.

I couldn't smile. I'd prepared myself for the worst and didn't know what to do in the face of good news.

'How's your arm?'

'The cording is getting worse despite the exercises.'

'We need to get it moving so you can have radiotherapy. It's been almost two months since the first op. I'll refer you to the physiotherapist.'

'OK.'

Lisa took me to another room to check my wound. I burst into tears.

'What's going on?'

'I'm fine. It's nothing.'

'I don't believe you,' she said.

'It's just that I'm in so much pain. The skin on my chest wall is burning and I'm finding it hard to cope. I don't want to bother anyone.'

'Stay here.'

Lisa came back a few minutes later with a prescription from Amanda for a different painkiller. 'If this doesn't work, she's written to your GP telling them what to try next.'

It took another six weeks before I could get my arm over my head. My hair had started to grow back as a halo of pale-grey fluff and tiny eyelashes were starting to sprout. I was still updating my weekly blog and loved reading the comments. I'd had some wonderful feedback from doctors, nurses and patients who were hooked on my double life. Every time I sent out a new post, it helped me distance myself from everything that was happening. Part of me was still in denial.

One day a group of medical students from King's College London got in touch. They were about to start their advanced communication skills module with a section on breaking bad news. It's not an area that trainees get a lot of exposure to, and they asked if I would come and talk to them to help them get it right. They'd read an early blog in which I'd talked about the power of language and were keen to know more.

I instantly said yes but I was nervous. It would be my first time talking in public since my diagnosis and I didn't want to let them down. I didn't want to talk about breast cancer treatment in detail as that was too specific for their stage of training. But then I thought about everything I'd noticed since I became a patient. Perhaps if I talked about the little things that had previously passed me by, I could help them understand what their patients might need in the future.

It was pouring with rain when we arrived in London. The cold February air hit me when I left the train. I wondered how many students would brave the elements to come and hear what I had to say. Dermot gave my hand a squeeze before we entered the lecture theatre. There were about forty people inside and you could hear a pin drop as I walked down the stairs to the front of the room. The student organising the event rushed up to shake my hand and introduced me to her friends. I took a deep breath, glanced at Dermot for luck, and then I began.

I could feel the energy in the room as they hung on my every word. The students had so many pertinent questions that made me stop and think about how I'd practised surgery before I became a patient. What would

I do differently? Would it make me a better surgeon? I didn't have the answers yet, but it was definitely food for thought. I could have talked for hours but it was getting late and we had to catch our train home. I turned to get my coat and saw Dermot had tears in his eyes. Everyone stood and clapped as I left. Just knowing that I'd been able to help them understand what it was like to be a patient gave me a sense of purpose again.

A few weeks later, it was time to start the run section of my cancer triathlon. West Suffolk didn't have a radiotherapy department so all my treatments would be done at Addenbrooke's in Cambridge. My first session was a planning CT scan so Dr Moody could accurately pinpoint which areas to target. I felt ashamed that I'd never seen a radiotherapy machine before. It was hard sitting by myself in the waiting room. I was no longer the youngest patient and my heart went out to the teenager sitting next to me. I couldn't cope with the fact that children had to go through this as well.

Once I was called through, two male therapeutic radiographers positioned me on the table. I felt so vulnerable as I lay there topless with both arms above my head. Although I'd got used to stripping off for Amanda, this was different. They were so caring and did their best to make me feel at ease. After the scan, I had to be tattooed. Three tiny black dots were scratched into my skin, one at the bottom of my cleavage and two on either side of my ribcage. Lasers would be lined up with the marks to make sure that I was in the same position for every treatment.

I was having my chest wall and the lymph nodes above

my collarbone treated and needed fifteen sessions over three weeks. The radiotherapy room was freezing. I got into position and the radiographer placed a blanket over my legs to keep me warm. The table I was lying on slowly moved into the machine. I looked up at the cartoon stickers above me that had obviously been placed there for children to stare at and felt a tear roll down my cheek. And then the machine kicked into action. It sounded like a giant mouse pushing a shopping trolley on gravel. A few minutes later and it was all over.

I was told it would take a couple of weeks to notice the side effects. My skin might turn red like sunburn and blister, leaving a permanent brown discoloration underneath. I could feel tired as the weeks went by. I was still recovering from chemotherapy and it was hard to hear that I might have another couple of months of feeling exhausted all the time. I remembered the patient who'd made a complaint about feeling drained after radiotherapy and realised this wasn't just the simple X-ray treatment I used to tell my patients about after all.

I soon got into a routine, but the travelling took its toll. It was a three-hour round trip. Dermot was able to take me for some of the sessions but I had to go alone for most of them. My skin became red and sore, I had bad indigestion and it was painful to swallow. I could only manage small mouthfuls of food at a time and couldn't drink anything too hot or too cold. After the last session I drove home in a daze. I'd made it through nine months of gruelling cancer treatment. I'd got so used to being seen by a doctor every couple of weeks and I wondered how I would feel now I was left to my own devices.

Sadly, my triathlon of treatment didn't earn me a medal at the end. Instead, it came with the menopause – a side effect of the tamoxifen Dr Moody had prescribed that I'd be taking for the next ten years to stop the cancer coming back. Instead of several years of a perimenopause that women naturally go through, mine would happen in a matter of weeks.

I read the information leaflet that came with the tablets. The list of symptoms caused by a lack of oestrogen was never-ending, including the risk of endometrial cancer, blood clots in my legs and a stroke. It was hard to get my head around the fact that I was now technically cancer-free yet would have to take a tablet for ten years that could make me feel rotten and might kill me. I was meant to accept all of this and be grateful to be alive. Dr Moody also wanted me to have Zoladex injections every month for five years, which would switch off my ovaries to further reduce the amount of oestrogen in my bloodstream. As a medical student, I'd seen an elderly man with prostate cancer have the injection. The needle was huge, as large as the brown venflons I used to put in trauma patients. It injected a small pellet into the stomach fat. The injections were given at my GP surgery. I'd had enough of needles and asked the locum doctor if I could have some local anaesthetic cream to numb my skin before it went in. She told me I'd be fine as it was only a scratch. How did she know? She'd never had it.

I made an appointment with the practice nurse. She took one look at me and said, 'Oh no, not another skinny one.'

There wasn't much fat to grab. The injection hurt like

hell but it was over in seconds and I was left with a massive bruise that took a week to settle down. Two weeks later the menopause ramped up a gear. I felt constantly sick and had a headache that wouldn't shift. The water retention in my ankles and calves meant it was a struggle to get my jeans off when I went to bed. I had hourly hot flushes and night sweats, and the stains on the mattress grew larger. My libido disappeared overnight. I hated what my life had now become.

I'd never appreciated how the drugs I'd handed out like smarties could ruin women's lives. I found it hard to move on when tamoxifen was a daily reminder of everything that had happened, and there were many times when I thought about flushing it down the toilet instead. Why had no one done any research to help with the side effects?

I avoided looking in the mirror. When I did, I could only focus on the negatives. The grey wiry fuzz on my head. The tight capsule around the implant that pulled my nipple upwards and outwards, forming ripples over the skin. The pubic hair and eyebrows that had forgotten where they were meant to grow and were having a free-for-all. Chin hairs that appeared overnight. I now turned away from Dermot as I undressed to get into bed. I couldn't let him see what cancer had done to me. I didn't want him to touch me. I felt so guilty that I couldn't respond the way I used to.

One night I was crying and Dermot woke up. He curled around me and asked, 'What's wrong?'

'I hate what cancer is doing to our marriage.'

'I know. But it's early days. We'll get through this.'

'I'm not sure we should. I'm giving you a way out.'

'What are you talking about?'

'I think you should divorce me and go and marry a woman with two breasts and a healthy libido to match.'

He sat up and looked at me.

'I'm not going anywhere. In sickness and in health, remember? You'd do the same if it was the other way around.'

I let my blog lapse. I'd finished treatment and I felt I had nothing left to say. Besides, it was time to start thinking about going back to work. I talked to Occupational Health and my GP and they'd both agreed I should take a good four to six months to recover first. It wasn't just the physical toll of treatment or the emotional stress of dealing with a cancer diagnosis. I had to prepare myself for the psychological impact of being a breast surgeon, having been a patient myself. I let my line manager know and agreed to get in touch at the end of the summer to start preparing my phased return. Meanwhile, I was going to throw myself into cycling.

Last July, Dermot had flown to Italy to cycle the Maratona event. It's a huge sportive in the Dolomites and thousands of riders flew from all over the world to take part. He was buzzing when he came back. Although I was jealous of the beautiful cycling jersey and gilet that were given to every rider, I needed that medal. It was enormous. We'd both signed up to do it during chemotherapy hoping I would be fit enough to get round the short course. It was now time to find out.

Dermot was going to stay with me the whole way

round. It was only fifty-five kilometres long but it was all up and down, with an altitude gain of almost two thousand metres. It was hard work grinding up the hairpin bends but the views made up for it. Seeing the mountains in the glorious sunshine made me feel alive again. We held hands as we rode across the finish line. I was so proud of myself and my new medal. I couldn't wait to do it again next year.

Back home, I started to plan my next triathlon. I had my sights set on a half-Ironman in the UK the following summer. It involved a 1.2-mile swim, a fifty-six-mile bike ride followed by a half-marathon. The distances were scary but I needed the challenge. I found a new triathlon coach, Tanja, who had trained her own dad during treatment for pancreatic cancer, and she believed she could get me round the course safely. This was not going to be about fast times and wondering how good I was in my age group. I had to look after my battered immune system and give my body time to recover properly. I couldn't wait to start.

Chapter 24

At the end of July, I saw Amanda for my annual follow-up and told her how painful my implant had become.

'I can take you back to theatre and release the capsule to see if that helps.'

'Can we wait a few months?' I said. 'I've had enough of hospitals for the moment.'

'Of course. Just let me know when you're ready.'

My mammogram was normal and she discharged me until my five-year appointment. Dr Moody did the same when I saw her a month later. It was now up to me to look out for signs of a recurrence. I was scared. Even with all the knowledge I had, would I know whether a cough was a just a cough or something more sinister? For the first couple of weeks I lay in bed at night running my hands over my body searching for lumps, paranoid that I might miss something.

Over the last six months I'd become good friends with a doctor called Trisha Greenhalgh. She was a GP and a professor at Oxford University. I had memorised one of her books about statistics to help me pass my final surgical exams and then one day during chemo she sent me a message to say that she was being treated for breast cancer as well. Like me, she had been desperate for more information about what it would be like to have breast cancer treatment. We shared our tips for constipation and bleeding piles and she told me about the things she'd read on patient forums. I was shocked when I heard that women were asking if their husband's hair would fall out if they had sex during chemo, or whether radiotherapy would make you radioactive.

Trish thought we should put all our knowledge to good use and write a book about breast cancer. We wanted people to understand what treatment was being offered and why, to share their fear and anxiety, having been through it ourselves, and hopefully make it less scary for them. I had no knowledge of the publishing world, but I put together a book proposal and sent it off to several agents. One replied within days. A couple of months later we'd signed a contract and could start fleshing out the chapters. I loved getting lost in the research and it was a great distraction from my painful implant.

I met with the new Ipswich medical director at the end of August to discuss going back to work. He said that most people took a month to build up to full-time work after a period of sick leave, but I didn't think that was anywhere near long enough. Besides, I was now legally disabled and I knew the Trust had to make reasonable adjustments to allow me to safely return. I reminded him that I'd had the same cancer as my patients and chemotherapy was a little more taxing than a pregnancy.

Also, I wasn't sure whether I was psychologically safe to operate.

My colleagues needed to know that I was competent to return as a surgeon. If I was still a trainee, it would have been easy to ask them to carry out the various assessments that were needed to progress to the next stage. However, there was no tool to ascertain whether a consultant was safe to work. It was left to the individual to decide, and I'm not sure I could. The medical director wasn't sure whether my own colleagues could, either. They knew me too well to give an unbiased judgement.

He reached out to the breast unit at Addenbrooke's, who agreed to take me on for six months as a part-time supernumerary consultant. They would observe me in clinics and theatres, check that my knowledge was up to date and ensure I was able to run departmental meetings and make difficult decisions. A long list of competencies was drawn up and I would have to pass each one before I could return to Ipswich as a consultant in my own right. I had no idea that it was going to take another six months for everything to be finalised.

While I was waiting for the final arrangements to be made, I was invited to give a TEDx talk in Stuttgart in September. I didn't actually know what a TED talk was, and after a few minutes looking at videos online I soon realised this was a big deal. They assigned someone to mentor me and he completely changed the way I prepared a talk. He told me that the German audience wouldn't care that I'd had breast cancer. I had to give them something useful to take away afterwards. It took three months to nail my script and memorise it. I'm sure I drove Dermot mad as I walked around the house in circles going over and over each line.

I based the talk around my jar of joy and asked the organisers if I they could get me an empty goldfish bowl to use as a prop. They went one better than that. At the end of my talk it was taken to the bar with a stack of cards and pens so the audience could fill it during the interval. When everyone came back, the host started pulling out entries to read and it was incredible to feel the room fill with joy.

I took the cards home and a friend translated them for me. Some were about passing exams and graduating or not getting stuck in traffic on the way to the theatre, but most were about simple pleasures. Spending time with loved ones, reuniting with old friends, making new friends, eating great food, having great sex. Halfway through the pile I pulled out a card that said: '*My boyfriend asked me to marry him after fourteen years. I said "Yes".*' I couldn't help but smile. And then, to my surprise, the very last card said: '*After fourteen years, she said "Yes".*'

Winter came and the pain from my implant switched up a gear. It was impossible to find a bra that didn't hurt and that fitted me properly. In the end I resorted to padded crop tops to stop my solitary nipple poking through my clothes. To make things worse, I now had regular spasms in the muscle covering the implant that made me swear out loud in pain. It was hard to remember why I'd had a reconstruction in the first place.

———

The following spring, Addenbrooke's were finally ready for me. I was desperately nervous. I had no idea how I was going to cope when I saw a breast cancer patient for the first time. I would be shadowing consultants who had trained me ten years ago. Could I now work alongside them as their equal, challenging their opinions and standing up for what I thought was best for the patients? There was only one way to find out.

I started with a symptomatic clinic and tagged along with one of the breast care nurses to find my feet. The next day I shadowed one of the consultants while he told a woman in her fifties that she had cancer. I was trying to concentrate on what he was saying but all I could focus on was the woman in front of me. I saw her face crumple as she heard the news. I watched her husband squeeze her hand before swearing under his breath. She gulped and prepared herself to hear what would happen next. I kept picturing how Dermot and I must have looked when we found out. It was too much. I made my excuses and left the room.

The next week I assisted another consultant with a mastectomy. He wanted me to do part of the case but I wasn't ready. It was hard enough holding a retractor. All I could imagine was what the woman under the drapes would feel when she came around. I could picture myself in her shoes, hoping that she wouldn't end up with the pain I had. I had never sutured a wound so carefully as I did that day.

A couple of weeks later, it was my turn to break bad news. I'd seen all the consultants do it and had a reasonable memory of what I used to say. The patient was already in the room and I'd hadn't had time to go through her notes properly before the consultant ushered me in. A beautiful young woman in her thirties was sitting waiting for me. Her results were bad. The lymph nodes were involved and she needed chemotherapy. All I wanted to do was give her a hug and tell her she would get through it. It took all the strength I had to remain professional. As soon it was over I fled to the toilets. What on earth was I thinking? There was no way I could be a breast surgeon again. I was reliving my diagnosis every time I saw a patient. I didn't want to operate because I was scared of how much pain I might cause.

The next week I had to tell a single mum in her forties that she had cancer. Her son was living overseas with his grandmother while she looked for work, and she'd come alone to the appointment. I did it as gently as I could. She crumpled in her chair, sobbing uncontrollably. Acting on instinct, I crouched down next to her, held her hand and said, 'I know it feels like the end of the world right now. It is shit, but we'll help you get through this.'

I was buzzing when I came out the room. I thought I'd done a great job in comforting her. I turned to the consultant and breast care nurse and knew something was up.

'You can't tell a patient that breast cancer is bad,' said the consultant. 'We need to be positive.'

'But I know how she feels. She was crying. What else was I meant to do?'

I was given extra training in how to break bad news from one of the radiologists who regularly taught students, and it was hard to accept that my new way of thinking might be wrong. It was going to take a lot of hard work when I went back to Ipswich. I'd have to ask my own breast care nurses to keep me in check and tell me when I overstepped the line. It did get easier as the months went by. The mask went back on.

In May, I noticed a couple of lymph nodes in the back of my neck. They were on the left, the same side as my cancer. I thought they were probably enlarged because of the bad cold I'd had over Easter but they got bigger as the weeks went by. A sick feeling crept into the pit of my stomach. I knew this wasn't a typical presentation of a recurrence but it didn't stop me worrying. I had an appointment to see Amanda the following week to talk about surgery to fix the implant. The night before I saw her, I found a huge lymph node in my right armpit. Now I was worried.

Amanda arranged an ultrasound and a CT scan for the following week. Although I felt relief that she was looking into my symptoms, the fear of what the scan might show was hard to bear. I'd read that cancer patients called it scanxiety but I'd never experienced it myself, until now.

My neck looked normal but the radiologist took a biopsy of the node in my armpit. I knew that meant it looked suspicious. As my mind went through the implications of my cancer coming back, I went to have the CT scan. I'd forgotten how the intravenous contrast makes you think that you've wet yourself. I felt a rush of warmth deep in my pelvis as it went in and had to check that the table was dry at the end. One week later I got the all-clear and Amanda booked me in for an implant revision at the end of October, when my time at Addenbrooke's would be over.

The following week I was pottering in the garden trying to keep on top of the weeds when I saw a flicker of movement at the back of the border. I slowly edged closer and saw a baby hedgehog. I knew it shouldn't be out in the day, so I gently picked it up and took it inside. There were a couple of cardboard boxes by the back door waiting to be taken to the dump. I made a nest out of some newspaper and gave it some cat food and water. The first three rescue shelters I rang were full, but then I found a tiny local one that had space. It was run by Ann and Chris, a couple in their seventies who cared for poorly hedgehogs in their house and garage until they were well enough to be released into the wild. My little hoglet was full of lungworm and ringworm and Ann quickly injected it with drugs. I felt like a superhero for saving its life and it was all I could talk about for days. Now I had to add hedgehog food to the shopping list along with suet pellets for the birds.

While I waited for my return to work to be finalised, I distracted myself with the challenge of adding to my medal collection, starting with the half-Ironman I'd been training for. It was a logistical nightmare getting my kit ready the day before. The swim and the start of the bike course were in a separate location to the run, which meant several trips back and forth checking I'd not for-gotten anything at either end. Dermot was going to cycle to cheer me on from the bike course but he got up at 5 a.m. to give me a hug before I made my way to the start. There were people everywhere and the atmosphere was electric. Disco music was blasting out and the compere was doing his best to keep our nerves at bay. In the middle of that huge crowd, however, I felt completely alone. As I lined up ready to jump into the dark water, I felt overwhelmed by everything I had been through and the race that lay ahead. A woman next to me gave me a hug and told me I'd get through this. She held my hand as we walked down the gantry. The gun went off and it was time to swim.

It was a beautiful morning without a cloud in the sky. I got into a rhythm and started to enjoy myself. Half an hour later I was running to get my bike. No one cared about modesty in the changing tents. I stripped off my wetsuit, put on my cycling kit, and was off. It was a hilly course and I needed to get round in four hours, leaving me three hours to walk the half-marathon if I was struggling. It was getting hotter as the day went on and I poured water over my head at every feed station. I heard Dermot cheer as I ground my way up a steep bit, determined not to stop. I made it with five minutes to spare. I had this. All I had to do was run.

I changed again into my running kit complete with a neon-pink tutu and a matching wig. I hate the colour pink. I'd decided to raise money for a breast cancer charity and had said that I'd wear fancy dress if I got over £2,000. My total was closer to £3,000, and I was starting to regret it. It was now over thirty degrees in the shade and I had a hilly three-lap course to cover. There was sweat dripping down my forehead thanks to the wig. The only reason I got around each lap was the crowds. They lined the streets, and as music blared from the pubs that we passed, they showered us in water from hosepipes and buckets. The first time I ran past, I heard a man shout, 'Let's hear it for the fairy!' I waved my arms in the air and twirled and danced all the way down the hill as they clapped and cheered. My coach Tanja had come down to cheer me on, and Dermot had bumped into her near the finish line. It was so good to see them. As I turned the final corner, judging my speed so I'd have the red carpet to myself for the photograph, I couldn't stop smiling. I had done it with fifteen minutes to spare. One year after finishing treatment.

A week later, Dermot and I flew to Italy to ride the Maratona and it was just as magical as before. Three weeks after that, we did the Ride 100 again on our new tandem. It was such fun being able to wave at everyone as we went past, although I did get a little tired of people yelling 'She's not pedalling'. I had one more challenge lined up before my surgery: a two-mile swim in the Serpentine in London. It was part of a new event called the London Classics. To get the medal, you had to have completed the London Marathon, the Ride 100 and this swim, and I needed that medal. It was huge, bigger than anything I had ever seen.

It was a chilly, wet September morning. The water was murky and cold and I was glad I was wearing my wetsuit, although many swimmers were braving it without one. It was a two-lap course and I was so tempted to quit after the first mile but I forced myself to keep going for another lap. I was shivering as I climbed out at the end and jumped straight into one of the waiting hot tubs so my hands and feet could defrost. And then I got my medals. Two: one for the swim and one for the triathlon. I couldn't stop looking at them on the train on the way home.

I was a lot more relaxed before surgery this time around. I'd be in and out in a day and didn't have the anxiety of cancer or results hanging over me. Amanda scored the capsule to split the thick ridges and replaced the implant. She also took some of the fat from my outer thighs and injected it above the capsule to even out the visible ripples and improve the quality of the skin. I felt like I'd been kicked by a horse when I woke up. Liposuction is a fairly brutal procedure and I had the bruises to prove it. She'd told me to wear knee-length Lycra support shorts for the next couple of months while I recovered at home, making my night sweats ten times worse. There was definitely no cuddling at night and it took several weeks before I stopped wincing every time I went up and down stairs. I used the time at home to concentrate on the last few chapters of the book I was writing with Trish.

I was now starting to worry about the practicalities of going back to Ipswich. I reached out to a coaching company called Working with Cancer and had a couple of sessions with a wonderful woman called Barbara. Although I knew how to treat patients, I hadn't thought about how to deal with colleagues. She helped me work through potential problems. What would I do when someone didn't recognise me now that I had short grey hair? What did I want everyone to know about the treatment I'd had? Did I want them to ask me how I was feeling or not mention it at all? How was I going to cope when I had to treat a particularly difficult case?

The final question I had to consider was whether I would be a better surgeon. I was often asked this and I was never sure what to say – I already thought I was good at my job. Most doctors have never had the illness they've been trained to treat and they still provide high-quality care. I was more concerned that it would make me a worse one. Could I shut out my own experiences as a patient when I desperately wanted to share them? Would I recommend chemotherapy when I knew the damage it could cause? If someone asked me 'What would you do, doctor?' should I answer them truthfully or guide them towards best practice? Only time would tell.

Chapter 25

As I drove over the bridge on my first day back at work, I kept remembering all those times I had thought about driving off it. All those days I had wanted to quit. How on earth was I going to cope now that I was a patient myself?

The day started with the departmental meeting where all the results were discussed, and the team agreed an individualised treatment plan for each patient before seeing them in clinic later that day. I sat back and listened as the pathologist read out the first case. 'She's a forty-two-year-old lady with a twelve-centimetre lobular cancer and three positive lymph nodes.'

'Shit. That's not good,' said one of the oncologists.

I listened to my colleagues talk about how bad the prognosis was for this woman. They could have been talking about me. She was a couple of years older and her cancer was a little bit smaller but that was it. It was all I could do not to burst into tears. I knew we needed to talk frankly in the meeting, but now I was a patient, it was painful to hear.

It is always difficult telling someone they have cancer, but now it was even harder. Part of me wanted to share my own experiences from when I was diagnosed, but I had to remain professional. There was only one patient in the room, and it couldn't be me.

I'd spent a lot of time thinking about the way I broke bad news. I used to tell women they were lucky we'd caught their cancer early and that it was good it hadn't spread. Because I'd seen the very worst of breast cancer, I wanted to reassure them that things weren't as bad as they might think. Now I had been on the other side, I questioned whether 'lucky' and 'good' were the right words to use. I relived my own experiences every single time I did it.

One day, one of the general surgeons walked past my door when I was in clinic. He knocked and came in.

'Hi. You must be one of the new consultants. I'm Mr Jenkins.'

'You don't recognise me, do you? It's Liz.'

He paused for a second, staring at my face until he worked out who I was.

'Oh God, I'm so sorry.'

'It's OK. I forget I look a little different these days.'

Getting through an operating list was the final hurdle I had to overcome to feel like I had any chance of returning to life as a breast surgeon. I'd cherry-picked simple cases for my first list and allowed myself a lot of time to do them. It was a lovely surprise when I walked into theatres and saw Chris and Val waiting for me. They gave me a huge hug and it felt like I'd come home again.

Instead of sitting in the coffee room while the anaesthetist put the first patient to sleep, I stayed in theatre and held her hand. It had meant so much to me when Amanda did it. One of the anaesthetic assistants asked me what I was doing.

'I'm just holding her hand.'

'That's my job,' she said.

After scrubbing up, I plastered on a smile and steadied myself to make the first cut. I turned to the anaesthetist and asked, 'Are you happy?'

'Yes,' she said.

'Knife, please.'

And I was off. It was just like riding a bicycle. My hands knew what to do. I had to forget about the woman on the table and just focus on the surgery. Before I knew it, both cases were finished with time to spare. I could do this.

One thing I wanted to try to improve was how I dealt with the gynaecological symptoms of the menopause. With some of the younger women I trusted my gut and told them that I knew how they were feeling because I was taking tamoxifen as well. I shared the tips that had helped me cope. I had no idea if I was doing the right thing ethically but there was no one else in the room to pass judgement. Most of the time it felt like it was the right choice.

It was incredibly tiring to have to make crucial decisions during the day after a year of just thinking about what to cook for supper, and I was getting more and more exhausted as the weeks went on. But by the time spring came around I was feeling better. I had proper days off when I didn't look at my laptop and work was easier as a result. I put the mask on to deal with patients at work and took it off again when I got home. I was back on my bike, training to do the Maratona again in

July, and weekends were spent walking Hunter by the coast or cycling to a pub on our tandem. The only fly in the ointment was my new implant. The capsule release hadn't worked and the pain was just as bad as before. I was now ready to go flat and get rid of it once and for all.

I made an appointment to see Amanda in May with a view to having surgery in the summer. I saw one of my own mastectomy patients in clinic that morning. For the first time I saw her scar through the eyes of a patient, not a surgeon. Although she was pleased with the result and had got used to wearing a prosthetic in her bra, all I could see was the absence of a breast. How would I ever get used to looking down and seeing nothing?

Amanda talked through what she was going to do and then examined me. She ran her fingers over a nodule of tissue at the lateral end of my mastectomy scar.

'How long has this been there?'

'About two years. I've been having physio on it every two to three weeks to try and free things up and keep my arm moving.'

'Let's get an ultrasound.'

'Are you worried?'

'No, but I'd rather be safe than sorry.'

I found myself back on the radiologist's couch as she scanned my chest wall. The first view looked completely normal but when she turned the probe something caught her eye.

'I'm just going to take a biopsy.'

Everything went into slow motion. I hadn't been expecting this. Amanda came in to see what was going on.

'It's probably just a nodule of scar tissue,' she said.

I didn't believe her. I had a sixth sense that it was going to be bad.

I went to outpatients to tell Dermot what had happened. He hadn't been able to go with me as he had his own clinic to run.

'I've had a biopsy.'

'Shit. Are you OK?'

'Just a bit sore.'

'Did she say what she thinks it is?'

'Probably just scar tissue. Better safe than sorry. Anyway, I just wanted you to know. See you at home?'

This time I didn't tell anyone at work what had happened, not even Sally. If I admitted it out loud it was real, and I wasn't ready to deal with the fact that my cancer might have come back. It was so hard getting through results clinics and hearing metastatic patients discussed in meetings. Would that be me in a few weeks' time?

I had an operating list the day before I got my results. I was completely wired and had barely slept. I'd waited until Dermot was asleep and then devoured cancer blogs. I knew it was the worst thing I could do but I couldn't stop. My normal registrar was on annual leave and a locum was standing in. I'd never met him before and he wouldn't stop talking. Normally I loved teaching but today was not the day. The first case was a simple lumpectomy and I got through it on autopilot. The second case was a wire-guided procedure in a very fatty breast. I couldn't feel the lump and the heat from the diathermy melted her tissue away as I cut down to find the wire.

The locum kept asking me what I was doing and I snapped. 'Not now. I need to concentrate.'

My scrub nurse raised her eyebrows above her mask. I'd never shouted in theatre before and my team knew it.

'Are you OK?'

'Yes,' I said. 'It's just hard to find, that's all.'

Eventually, I got the cancer out but I couldn't remember which way up it went. If I got it wrong and the margins were positive it would be a disaster. She could end up having more tissue taken from the wrong area, potentially leaving cells behind. I marked it as best I could and apologised to the locum. I knew I shouldn't have done the list. I should have told one of my colleagues what was happening and asked them to cover for me. I'd thought I'd be fine. I was wrong.

Dermot was on-call that evening. He came home at midnight but was disturbed by hourly phone calls before going back in again at 5 a.m. to operate. Neither of us got much sleep. I was almost sick in the car as I drove myself from my own outpatient clinic as a doctor to my results clinic as a patient. The clinic was running late and Dermot was still seeing patients on the ward. I sat by myself in the waiting room surrounded by anxious couples. I kept my head down so I couldn't make eye contact with the clinic staff. They would have all been in the meeting earlier that day when my results were discussed and I didn't want to find out in the waiting room because of the way they looked at me.

Dermot arrived just as my name was called. Before Amanda said anything, I knew. I could see it in her eyes.

'It's cancer, the same as before.'

I felt Dermot grip my hand.

'From the ultrasound it's about two and a half centimetres.'

I stopped listening after that. This couldn't be happening. How had I not known what it was? Amanda passed me a tissue and I tried to focus on what she was saying.

'You're going to need a CT and a bone scan to check it isn't anywhere else. I've booked you in for surgery in two weeks. I'll take the implant out and try to make the scar as neat as I can.'

For the third time in three years, Dermot and I found ourselves crying on that bench. Despite chemotherapy, radiotherapy, surgery and tamoxifen, my cancer had come back, and quickly. My brain couldn't cope with the numbers flying around my head. If it had spread elsewhere, I had an average of three years left to live.

'How bad is it?' Dermot asked.

'I don't know yet,' I said. 'I'll have a better idea when the scan results are back.'

He rang a colleague to ask if they could cover his on-call for the rest of the week and we went home to tell our families.

Thankfully, my scans were normal and it was only a locoregional recurrence on my chest wall. The ten days I spent waiting for my operation were even harder than the first time around. As well as getting my head around the recurrence, I had to prepare myself for going flat. Although I hadn't worn a bra for over a year because of the neuropathic pain on my chest wall, I would now need one for the prosthesis. I went into a local department store and ended up bursting into tears. There was nothing in my size. It was as if lingerie manufacturers didn't think women with small breasts had mastectomies. A lovely assistant came over, gave me a hug and showed me a bra online that might work. There was only one choice. And it was pink. I went home and ordered one. I then stroked the long dresses in my wardrobe that I'd no longer be able to wear before stuffing them in a suitcase. I couldn't bear to look at them. They reminded me of the body I used to have.

I was a nervous wreck on the morning of the surgery. I'd managed to hold it together while I got into my gown and Amanda and the anaesthetist came to see me, but once the porters arrived I started to panic. Dermot had nipped back to his office to sort out a few things and I begged them to wait just a couple of minutes so I could say goodbye. He came back in the nick of time and I sobbed into his shoulder as we held each other tightly.

The operating room wasn't quite ready so I was wheeled into a holding area to wait. Once the curtain was pulled around me the floodgates opened. I didn't want to have cancer. I didn't want it to come back. I didn't want to die because of it. A lovely nurse popped her head in and offered me a bunch of tissues before taking me into theatre.

As usual, Amanda held my hand while I drifted off to sleep. I woke up on the ward but couldn't bear to look down at my chest. A couple of hours later Amanda came to see me. It had gone well, but she'd had to leave my nipple behind. Previous radiotherapy meant the skin wouldn't stretch enough for her to remove it and close the wound. She peeked inside my gown to check for bleeding. I stared up at the ceiling. I still needed time. Lisa gave me a soft 'comfy' to put in my bra for the first couple of months, and then it was time for Dermot to take me home.

I had to get changed into normal clothes in order to leave the hospital and I couldn't put it off any longer. As I took off my gown, I looked down at the long white dressing over the wound. Beneath that dressing would be an ugly scar with a shrivelled nipple sitting above it. One week later I was back in clinic for a wound check. As Lisa peeled back the dressing I looked at my flat chest for the first time and saw an ugly, wrinkled, tethered scar. My shrivelled nipple had been pulled over towards my armpit. Previous radiotherapy meant the skin wouldn't stretch and this is what I was left with. I just felt so sad at everything I thought I'd lost. My femininity. My sexuality. My future.

I went home and put on the bra with the soft prosthesis inside. I lasted about four hours until I had to take it off because of the pain. The reality hit me that I was going to be lopsided forever. I spent hours online over the next few days looking for clothes that would disguise my disfigured shape. I found several tops with ruffles and frills but they were all on the wrong side. I would just have to live in baggy jumpers all summer long so no one would stare at my chest.

Up until then I'd been sleeping with a T-shirt on but I would wake up drenched in sweat from the hot flushes. That night I decided it was time to let Dermot see what his wife now looked like. I was so scared. As I took off my top I had to fight the urge to cover my scar with my hands.

'You're beautiful.'

'You don't need to say that.'

'I mean it. You are. I love you. And anyway, I didn't marry you because of your breasts.'

The next day a breast cancer charity got in touch. They sponsored one of the jerseys for the women's cycling Tour of Britain and were asking patients to write inspirational messages for the riders. These were then written on to pink ribbons that the cyclists wore during the race. I was thrilled to be chosen and quickly replied. They then asked me if I would like to present their jersey to the winning rider at the stage that finished in Suffolk. I jumped at the chance.

They'd arranged for me to watch the start of the race in the VIP area. I got to talk to my cycling heroines as they went past to sign on. It was so wonderful to see the ribbons plaited in their hair and wrapped around their handlebars and to tell them how much it meant to me. A few of them got emotional when they found out that I'd had cancer. They said that they rode for us and it pushed them to ride harder. The race was exhilarating to watch and it was such an honour to present the jersey to the rider with the most points. I then found out that the cyclist who'd won the 'Queen of the Mountains' jersey was wearing my ribbon. I plucked up the courage to introduce myself and she insisted I take the cuddly toy and flowers she'd been given on stage. It had been the perfect day.

Two days later I got my results. Although the cancer itself was the same size as the scan had shown, Amanda hadn't been able to remove it completely. She'd taken all the tissue she could but the margin closest to my ribcage had cancer cells in it. Without a clear rim of tissue, the odds of another recurrence were high.

'You won't need chemotherapy again. There's no evidence that it works for local recurrences.'

'That's a relief.'

'I'll need to switch you to letrozole and put you back on Zoladex until you're fully menopausal.'

'Could I have my ovaries out instead? I hate the injections.'

'It is an option. I'll ask one of the gynaecologists to see you, but you'll need to have Zoladex in the meantime.'

'OK.'

'Finally, Dr Moody thinks that it might be worth giving you more radiotherapy.'

'But I've already had a full course. I didn't think you could give it again?'

'Normally we don't, but it might be worth a shot. She'll see you next week to go through the details.'

I spent the next few days searching for information about a double dose of radiotherapy but came up empty-handed. I hated not knowing what was going on. Dermot managed to get someone to cover his clinic and we found ourselves sitting in the oncology waiting room again.

Dr Moody explained that the recurrence was in the area previously treated by radiotherapy. It could be given twice, but it was rarely done. She'd only given it a couple of times before and was only considering it because of the positive deep margin. The risk of cancer cells forming another recurrence was high and it would be a lot harder to resect. I didn't fancy having part of my ribcage removed.

She went on to say that the side effects could be far greater the second time around. The chronic pain on my chest wall could get worse. I could develop lymph-oedema. The scar tissue beneath my armpit could thicken and tether, further reducing my shoulder movement on that side. The skin around the wound could break down, needing a skin graft or a muscle flap to fill the hole. The nerves at the top of my armpit could be damaged, leading to permanent paralysis. It was a lot to take in.

Finally, she said that I could have the treatment, develop all of the side effects and the cancer could still come back. The fact that it had grown in an area that had previously been treated meant that the recurrence could be resistant to radiotherapy. I could end up with a painful, useless arm and metastatic disease.

'I don't know how to advise you. What do you want to do?'

How did I make a sensible decision? There were no trials. No real evidence. If the expert in front of me didn't know what to do then how was I expected to? My gut told me to walk away. I'd had enough. As I said no, Dermot said it was worth a try. Dr Moody stepped in.

'Why don't you have a think about it and let me know in a week or so?'

Later that night I tried to explain to Dermot how I felt. I'd had two years of chronic pain. I already had a stiff shoulder. There was a high chance that my quality of life would deteriorate if I had more radiotherapy. I might never be able to operate again. Ride a bike again. Tolerate a hug again.

'I understand,' he said, 'but I don't want you to die.'

I could see the tears in his eyes and it killed me.

'You're not the one who has to live with the consequences and be in constant pain,' I said. 'I don't want to hate you for forcing me to do this.'

In the end I did the only sensible thing I could think of. I arranged to see another oncologist, recommended by several people I knew. Dermot and I agreed before we went in that I'd do whatever she said. After looking through my notes and examining me thoroughly, she came straight to the point.

'It's a tough choice, but there's only one answer. You need to have more radiotherapy. If it was just a couple of cells at the margin, it would be a different story. But it's not. There's a chance it will work and I think you should take it.'

Decision made.

By the end of my fifteenth session, my skin had burned and blistered and I was exhausted. The cording had come back and I lived in baggy tops. I felt miserable and this was only after a few weeks. How bad would it be in six months' time?

Three weeks later I was back in theatre to have my ovaries removed. The anaesthetist gave me an epidural for the pain and I wanted to kiss her afterwards. I was numb from the ribcage down and for sixteen blissful hours I was pain-free for the first time in three years. I slept like a log overnight and although I woke up with raging hot flushes, I didn't care. I'd never have to have a needle in my stomach again.

I saw Simon in Occupational Health and he suggested I take three months to recover. It gave me breathing space to get my head around everything that had happened before I went back to work. Lisa rang to check how the surgery had gone and I burst into tears.

'Have you thought about counselling?'

'No,' I said.

'You're entitled to free sessions with the therapist in the oncology unit.'

Why had nobody told me this before? Sheila was one of the kindest women I have ever met. As I explained everything that had happened, she immediately understood how hard it had been for me to go back to work. I wanted to talk about how to cope as a breast surgeon again but she said, 'You're not ready. You still haven't come to terms with your own recurrence.'

Instead, we talked about everything that was keeping me awake at night. I told her how alone I felt. I didn't know anyone else who'd had the same recurrence and treatment. I was desperate for more information but I couldn't find any relevant papers or clinical trials. Then I said that some days I wanted my cancer to come back properly so I could stop the dreadful, endless waiting. I didn't mean it. No one in their right mind would want to get incurable cancer. I'd lost so many friends to metastatic disease and the guilt of being alive when they were no longer around was awful. However, the anxiety of dealing with the fear of another recurrence could be overwhelming at times. Finally, I admitted I was scared of dying.

'Remember,' she said, 'you've only seen traumatic deaths on the wards as part of a crash team. Most cancer patients will die peacefully, supported by palliative care.'

It helped a little, but I was still scared. I hadn't written a will or told Dermot what kind of funeral I wanted. Just the thought of finalising the end of my life was too big to deal with.

'But everyone dies,' she said. 'It's the one certainty in life. You can't change that.'

'I guess you're right.'

'You know I am. Getting your affairs in order and telling your husband whether you want to be buried or cremated is just common sense. Get it done and then you can put it behind you.'

In my next session, Sheila wanted to help me accept my body. I still walked around with my shoulders hunched and my head hung low to stop people staring at my lopsided chest.

'You do realise that no one is looking at you? Most of us are so hung up on our own body insecurities that we don't notice other people.'

She was right. Everyone has bits of their bodies they don't like.

'You have to stop beating yourself up. You're never going to get your breast back. You may never be able to wear a bra. But you're alive and there is so much you can do.'

I'd been so open about sharing my cancer diagnosis with the world so why did I want to hide how I looked? I didn't need to love my body, not yet, but I had to give it a break. I went home, stripped off and looked in the mirror. I forced myself to touch the scar and feel the cords running through my armpit and down my arm. I put on a T-shirt and looked again. Because my remaining breast was small, it wasn't that obvious that I only had one. I'd performed mastectomies on many women with huge breasts where it would have been far more noticeable. It was time to hold my head up high and accept my scars.

My left shoulder became more and more painful. I couldn't move my arm fully and the power wasn't there. I hid it well and tried not to complain all the time to Dermot. I kept busy and still cycled and swam when I could, but I was seriously worried that it would affect my ability to operate.

I continued to see Sheila and we talked about work. I told her how unhappy I'd been before my diagnosis and that the job had almost killed me. Putting my own cancer aside, could I really go back into that environment? And even if I did find a way to cope, could I deal with the emotional burden of cancer patients when I was still processing my own recurrence? I didn't think I could separate my own experiences from the women I was treating. How would I manage the fear and anxiety I would feel every time I diagnosed someone with metastatic disease? Finally, none of these questions mattered if I couldn't operate because of my shoulder.

'What does your gut say?' she asked.

'To walk away. It's too much. But what will I do if I'm not a surgeon anymore?'

'Whatever you like.'

I spent the weekend talking to Dermot about other possibilities.

'What about retraining in a different speciality?' he asked.

'I'd have to go back on the wards, which means being

on-call again and that's never going to happen. And even if I did, with the way my shoulder is, I doubt I'd be able to do anything but the simplest operation.'

We worked our way through other options that would let me keep working as a doctor but came up empty-handed. Surgery had been my life for the last twenty-six years. It was the reason I woke up in the morning. I'd dedicated myself to helping people the only way I knew how. And now, at the age of forty-five, my surgical career was over.

I remembered the last operation I'd performed. It hadn't gone smoothly and I'd shouted at the locum. I didn't leave the table on a high like I usually did. Would it have been different if I'd known that it was the last time? The last time I'd scrub up, or use a scalpel, or hold a patient's hand? I wiped the tears away and emailed Occupational Health to say that I was going to retire due to ill health.

Chapter 26

I had the rest of my life ahead of me and was scared about how little of it I might have left. It was hard not to imagine what might happen in the future, and every ache and pain made me think the worst. I spent hours on the sofa staring into space. The only reason I got out of bed in the morning was to walk the dog. I didn't have long to be maudlin because in a few weeks the book Trish and I had been slaving over for the past year would be published and there were articles to write and interviews to do. It had taken several months to settle on a title but *The Complete Guide to Breast Cancer: How to Feel Empowered and Take Control* was about to become a reality.

The publisher sent us some copies of our book a few days before it was released, and I felt so proud when I held it in my hands. How on earth had I achieved this after everything I had been through? I was anxious to find out if anyone would find the book useful and had to stop myself from checking Amazon every ten minutes. But over the next few days, people started leaving comments. One woman wrote: 'This book will hold your hand all the way through the next few months and years.

I wish I'd had this book earlier, right from my diagnosis.' A man emailed me to say thank you as he finally understood why his wife's sex drive had disappeared overnight. And then a surgeon in Australia told me she'd arranged charity funding so she could give a copy to all her patients. It felt so good to know that I could still help the breast cancer community even though I was no longer a surgeon.

When the excitement of the book launch settled down, I was lost. I missed the regular human contact I had at work and that feeling in the operating room at the end of a case. I was so lonely. Days would go by when the only words I said were 'Good boy, Hunter', and Dermot got frustrated with my verbal diarrhoea the minute he walked through the door. I started to slide into depression again. I spent hours doom-scrolling on my phone instead of facing up to the reality of my situation. Had I really got through breast cancer twice to spend my days like this?

I was still cycling, running and swimming when I could, but my heart wasn't in it. Although I still had dreams of completing an Ironman one day, deep down I just didn't like running. Saying it out loud lifted a huge weight from my back. I was only signing up for crazy sporting challenges because I thought people expected me to, and then I'd beat myself up when I had to pull out because I hadn't trained properly. So instead of forcing myself to run every weekend, I started volunteering at my local parkrun instead. I loved cheering everyone on as they went past and I went home on such a high.

It took four months for my ill-health retirement to be

approved. I was expecting to feel relief but when I opened the letter, I burst into tears. It suddenly hit me that I would never operate again. This was not how my career was supposed to end. The reality of life without a purpose was staring me in the face, and instead of taking my time to work out what I wanted to do, I rushed straight into another job. West Suffolk Hospital had set up a team to review the care of people who had died in the Trust. They needed another reviewer and I jumped at the chance. It was only one day a week and it was as close to being a doctor as I could get without retraining. What I didn't realise was just how hard it was going to be.

One of the first cases I reviewed was a woman in her forties who had died from metastatic breast cancer. Part of the job involved going to the mortuary to check that the body in the fridge belonged to the patient who had died. Marie was on duty and she pulled back the sheet so I could check the name band on the wrist. I lost it. All I could see was my own body lying there in the future. I started to cry. What on earth was I thinking when I signed up for this? Marie put the kettle on, and we sat and chatted about how she coped with it all. We soon became good friends and I learned to dissociate the body from the person I'd come to know from the notes. It was just like operating. The patient on the table became a lesson in anatomy or a logic problem so my emotions didn't affect my decision-making.

The hardest part of the job was talking to the relatives. It was horrible having to cold-call them and ask about the care. I spoke to one husband who was suicidal now that his wife of sixty years was no longer alive. He was broken. I was scared about what he might do when I hung up. I managed to find the number for the Samaritans so he had someone to talk to afterwards but it preyed on my mind for weeks. An angry daughter shouted at me for an hour because she hadn't been told just how ill her mother was. Another blamed me personally for killing her mother. It was worse than telling women they had cancer.

But it wasn't all bad. I read some wonderful cases, especially when the palliative care team were involved. One woman told me that they managed to get fish and chips for her father's final meal, and an elderly man with no relatives was given an iPad by a nurse so he could listen to country and western music when he was feeling lonely at night. It was those little things that kept me going. I hoped that by looking for the great things that had happened, I could help to improve care for everyone.

Meanwhile, the painkillers I was taking for my chronic pain stopped working and my cording came back with a vengeance. I couldn't take it anymore, so in desperation I reached out to Amanda. She referred me to the pain consultant, who suggested injecting Botox into the muscle. She said it might stop the muscle spasms for a couple of months and was worth a try. I hopped up on to the couch and pulled down my bra top. We were chatting away as she filled the syringe and then she said, 'Sharp scratch.'

'Ow! Shit, that's sore.'

'Sorry. It won't be for long.' She carefully prodded my knotted muscles and injected a small amount into each area. 'Let's see if it works.'

I looked like I'd been attacked by a vampire, with tiny puncture marks on my chest, and it was sore for a few days, but then the pain went away. For the first time in years, I didn't need to take painkillers.

Although the job at the hospital kept me occupied, it wasn't making me happy. Reading and talking about death with no other work to distract me was getting me down. I became more obsessed with my own death and how good or bad it might be, reliving those early days when I was first diagnosed. I wanted to quit, but I didn't want to tell Dermot. I felt a responsibility to try to earn some money now I wasn't bringing home a surgeon's salary. But more than that, I knew he would worry about how lonely I would be without a regular job. I kept going for another couple of months, but I began to dread the hours I would spend trawling through the notes. Every morning I would search for an excuse that would keep me at home. I had to tell Dermot how I felt.

'We need to talk.'

Dermot looked up from his phone. I still hadn't learned how to start these difficult conversations. 'I can't spend my days talking about death. It's not good for me.'

'I get it, you know I do, but what will you do instead?'

'I don't know. I need time to think. I just want to feel happy again.'

We were both nervous that my mood would drop, but that was on the cards if I stayed in the job. And so I handed in my notice. I was sad to say goodbye, but I knew it was for the best.

I spent hours looking for things I could do, and then I remembered the hedgehog I'd rescued. I knew that Ann relied on volunteers, and now I had some time on my hands, I wondered if she needed another one.

'I don't know if you remember me, but I dropped off a poorly hedgehog last year.'

'Have you found another one? I'm not sure we've got room for anymore.'

'That's not why I'm calling. Could you use another volunteer?'

'Of course. We're always looking for more help.'

Two days later I turned up for training. She taught me how to clean out the hedgehogs' plastic crates and make a nest out of newspaper for them to sleep in. It felt like I'd come full circle as I was back to working with shit again, but I did get to hold the baby hoglets. I never knew that their legs were so long or that their ears were so large, tucked away under their spines. It felt wonderful to give up my time to do something worthwhile for someone else, and it soon became a highlight of my week.

My days were quickly filled with preparing talks for a variety of conferences. I would sit in the kitchen with a mug of tea and my laptop. Hunter lay at my feet, pre-tending to sleep, hoping that a biscuit might find its way to the floor. I no longer got emotional when I told my story on stage, and that feeling of having a room full of people hanging on my every word was like a drug. I had lectures lined up months in advance and loved leaving doctors and nurses with little things they could do to immediately improve their patients' lives. Things like making sure someone in the team talked about sex after cancer or changing the words they used when they broke bad news. Things that I knew would have a huge impact on patient care. It was surreal that I could help far more people through public speaking than I ever did with a scalpel. Although I'd loved being in the operating room, most of my life as a surgeon was spent talking to patients in clinic. Now I was talking again, but this time on an equal footing with my audience. I loved being asked questions at the end of every session, and always came home buzzing with ideas about what else I could do to change the narrative around cancer care. Did I really need a proper job to make a difference?

As I stared at the blue tits on the feeder outside, my cup of tea now cold, I thought back to all those hours spent in the operating room. The laughter I'd shared, the bullying I'd endured, the flirting I'd enjoyed. When I was gowned and gloved, the only thing people could see was my eyes above the surgical mask. I didn't need to be in a power suit and heels to command the room. I didn't need a box of tissues to let someone know I was thinking about them. It didn't matter who I was or what I looked like. I went to the bathroom and stared at my reflection. I looked scared. Maybe that wasn't surprising. The cancer could come back at any time. I knew that better than anyone. But behind the fear, shining through, was hope. I still had more to give. I wiped away a tear. I didn't need a label. I was just Liz. And that was good enough for now.

Acknowledgements

One day I had an urge to share my story, warts and all, in the hope that it would help others in a similar situation. And now it's finally happened. But this book could not exist without the help, love and support of so many people.

To Dermot, the husband of this more-famous wife. Thank you for always being there, in sickness and in health. For your support, patience and for always believing in me. I could not have done this without you by my side. I love you.

To my family. You gave me the strength to power through when the shit kept hitting the fan. To Dad, for reading every draft and being my biggest fan, and to Nick and Jihane, for the Swiss chocolate and for bringing me back down to earth when I needed it. We all miss Mum. My heart still breaks when I remember that she won't get to hold a signed copy in her hands.

To my wonderful friends who have cheered me on, from near and far. In no particular order, to Judith, for the Wonder Woman mascot. To The Enablers, for the midnight rants, enabling (obviously) and filthy knitting. To Hannah, for sharing the trials of becoming an author over tea and cake. To Elaine, for the science stuff. To Ann, for the weekly hedgehog therapy. To Greg Wise and Kathryn Mannix, for the virtual cocktail writers support group. To Elizabeth, my back-bottom, for the no-nonsense advice, burgers and ego-stroking. And finally, to Daljit, for thirty years of true friendship, for stopping me falling down a black hole and for always being there for me, even when I think I don't need you.

To the writers who have inspired me. To Marcus, for giving me the power to reach down into the depths of my depression and put it on paper. To the Just Write Gang – our weekly Zooms have been a source of joy, laughter and inspiration. You have taught me so much, and one day I will learn how to kill someone on a train (for a book, before anyone starts to panic). Special thanks to Cathy Rentzenbrink who mentored me and showed me how to make magic on the page. You made me believe that I can actually write. I can't wait to swim in the sea with you.

To everyone who helped turn my memories into an actual book. To my agent Clare Hulton, for believing in my story despite the countless rejections. To Fiona Lens-velt, for sending me a DM after a desperate tweet and introducing me to the team at Unbound. To Cassie Waters, Alex Eccles, Rachael Kerr, Imogen Denny and Rina Gill for doing what you do so brilliantly. To Mark Ecob, for the incredible cover combining my love of sewing both people and clothes. And finally, to Alys Cole-King, for your sensitivity read to make sure my writing was safe for people to read. You were there for me when I was in a very dangerous place and I cannot thank you enough.

And finally, to everyone who took a chance on my story and helped make it happen. I had an inkling that I might reach my crowdfunding target in a couple of months, but to reach it in ten days is just bonkers. So thank you for following me, believing in me and for making my dream come true.

A Note on the Author

Liz went to medical school in Cardiff in 1998 and trained in South Wales and East Anglia for twenty years until she made it as a consultant breast surgeon in 2013. She spent her days treating women with breast cancer and loved her job. After getting breast cancer twice, she was forced to retire in 2018 and has been busier than ever forging a new career from her home in Suffolk.

She wrote *The Complete Guide to Breast Cancer: How to Feel Empowered and Take Control* (Vermillion, 2018) with Prof Trisha Greenhalgh to give women answers to all the questions she had as a patient. She speaks all over the world about resilience and how to improve patient care. Last year, she launched a podcast, *Don't Ignore the Elephant*, to help more people talk about taboos like sex and death.

Unbound is the world's first crowdfunding publisher, established in 2011.

We believe that wonderful things can happen when you clear a path for people who share a passion. That's why we've built a platform that brings together readers and authors to crowdfund books they believe in – and give fresh ideas that don't fit the traditional mould the chance they deserve.

This book is in your hands because readers made it possible. Everyone who pledged their support is listed below. Join them by visiting unbound.com and supporting a book today.

Sarah Anderson

Michelle Andrew

Agnieszka Andrzejak

Susan Angoy

Althea Armour

Alison Armstrong

Claire Armstrong

Gillian Ashley

Alex Ashman

Zoe Ashton

Patricia Ashworth

Linda Atkins

Michelle Atkinson

Jane Austin

Joanna Axam

Lauren Ayms

Megan Ayms

Jillian Aziz

Marianne Aznar

Alison Backhouse

Charlotte Badescu

Andrew Baildam

Stephen Bailey

Sarah Bainbridge

Jenny Baker

Kathryn Baker

Ruth Baker

Alison Baldock

Judith Baldwin

Maggie Baldwin

Louise Balhatchet

Isobel Ball

Jihane Ball

Keith Ball

Nicholas Ball

Philip Ball

Raphael Ball

Carol Barbeler

Alison Barnes

Melda Barnes

Amanda Barrett

Sue Barrow

Susan Bates

Eesther Batstone

Anna Baverstock

Olivia Beagan

Julie Beardmore

Gillian Beaton

Helen Bedford

Julie Bedwood

Rachael Beetham

Karen Beggs

Janet Bellis

Phillip Bennett-Richards

Cathryn Berry

Janet Berry

Sabine Best

Mahesh Bhandari

Lauren Bishop

Lisa Bishop

Denise Black

Elizabeth Black

Sue Blackburn
Vicky Blackburn
Shana Blackley
Michele Blackwood
Helen Blair
Alex Blakemore
Debbie Bliss
Jan Bloomfield
Kirstin Bloxam
Lyndsey Bloxsome
Rebecca
   Blunsom-Washbrook
Ruth Board
Jennifer Bonnie
Clare Bonthrone
Jo Boon
Kathryn Borrows
Helen Bostock
'Back Bottom'
Julia Bowden
Paul Boyle
Sarah Boyle
Faye Brady
Julie Braithwaite
Maria Bramley
Caroline Brennan
Lucy Brett
Claire Brewer
Clare Bridgestock
George Brighton
Anastasia Britten

Nicola Broderick
Katie Bromley
Caroline Brooke
Jan Browman Barnes
Carla Brown
Hannah Brown
Katherine Brown
Kirsten Brown
Marita Brown
Brian Browne
Beverley Bryant
Hannah Bryant
Karen Buckley
Christine Budd
Samantha Burge
Caroline J Burke
Jill Burrows
Patricia Bussy
Victoria Butler-Cole
Kit Byatt
Amy Byer Shainman
Pamela Byrne
Amelia Campbell
Nia Campbell
Jayne Camuglia
Aimée Canavan
Marie Cann-Livingstone
Niki Cannon
Gina Cantillon
Philip Caren
Catherine Cargill

Enitan Carrol
Carol Jane Carter
Laura Carvey
Jo-anne Casey
Tracy Catherall
Jonathan Cathie
Katrina Cathie
Lucy Cathie
Rosie Cathie
Sarah Cavanagh
Louise Cave
Neroli Chadderton
John Chapman
Pam Chappell
Liz Charlesworth
Mary Chavez
Helen Cheal
Anne Cheng
Cynthia Chewter
Korina Chisholm
Lotte Chitty
Alex Chiu
Dee Christie
Richard Chudleigh
Oana Circiu
Brenda Clark
Jane Clark
Adam Clarke
Alex Clarke
Emma Clarke
Justine Clarke

Melanie Clarke
Niamh Clarke
Traci Clarke
Joanne Clements
Birgit Cloos
Di Cocksedge
Liz Cohen
Alys Cole-King
Kate Comiskey
Bríd Conneely
Dr Claire Connolly
Stefanie Connoly
Ann Connor
Anita Cooper
Heather Cooper-Waite
Carolyn Corden
Anne Marie Cosgrave
Sarah Cotter
Jackie Cotter felow
    surviror
Tracy Cottis
Angela Cowell
Sonia Crandall
Rachel Crockett
Anne Cullen
Gel Cullen
Alexander Cunliffe
Denise Curti
Dr Kate Cushing
Ravi Cuttilan
Sonia Czak

Felecia D'souza
Eva D'Souza
Ning Daodao
Susan Darvey
Katrina Daskalogianni
Heather M Davidson
Janet Davics
Alice Davis
Dr Jessica Dawe
Wendy Day
Prinith De Alwis
  Jayasinghe
Mar Estupiñán Fdez.
  de Mesa
Nicola Deeth
Sharlene Deklerk
Debbie Denton
Judith Desprez
Nichiless Dey
Haryana Dhillon
Cheryl Dibbin
Paula Dicker
Polly Dickerson
Angela Dickson
Jane Dickson
Shannon Doggett
John Doherty
Brian Dolan
Kirsty Doole
Matthew Doré
Pascale Doria

Mary Dougan
Jennifer Douglas
Isla Dowds-Skinner
Aisling Doyle
Hilary Drain
Jane Duncan
Katy Dunn
Lily Dunn
Rohith E
Eran Edry
Anwen Edwards
Ginny Edwards
Rachel Edwards
Rachael Eizlini
Nicky Elkington
Rosanne Ellacott
Pat Ellerby
Patricia Elliott
Rachel Elliott
Roz Elliott
Kerry Elstob
Imogen Ely
Kate Emberson
Judit Etherington
Cindy Etherton
Lena Evans
Michelle Evans
Penny Evans
Diane Evans-Wood
Pia Fagelman
Carolyn Fahm

Eneas Faleiros
Patricia Faria
Sue Faulds
Lucy Fawcett
Patric ffrench Devitt
Alison Findlay
Susan Findlay
Joanne Finn
Sarah Fitzgibbon
Julie Fitzjohn
Susan Flannery
Clare Flexman
Caroline Flynn
Edward Fogden
Valerie fossey
Leigh Foster
Jane Fowler
Trish Fowlie
Hannah Fox
Mary-Ann Fox
Maxine Foy
Kerry Fraser
Edwina Freeman
Helen Friend
Mairi Fuller
Sasha Gabbe
Andrew Gabriel
Catherine Galvin
Joan Gandy
Elaine Gardener
Adele Gardner

Heidi Gardner
Sarah Garner
Carolyn Garritt
Siobhan Gaynor
Sarah Geer
Danielle Gibson
Carol Gilchrist
Michelle Gillett
Laura Ginesi
Stephanie Giorgio
Liberty Godwin
Edwina Goh
Julie Goldstraw
Kelvin Gomez
Ann Gorecki
Beverly Graham
Beckie Green
Sue M Green
Tracy Green
Aodhan Griffin
Rachael Griffin
Tracey Grinter
Noreen Guiney
Pallavi Gungadin
Gwen
Nadine Haasnoot
Agi Hajnal
Dorothy Halfhide
Nicola Hall
Sue Hall
Kathy Halligan

Becki Hamilton
Jane Harari
Carolyn Harlow
Kim Harman
Dr Tracey Harrington
Alice Harrison
Peter Harrison
Lisa Harvey
Catherine Hastie
Dirk Haun
Heather
Amanda Hembrough
Lisa Henderson
Karen Henry
Sonia Hibble
Moira Hickson
Rose Higgins
Elaine Hill
Stuart Hindle
Gwyneth Hinds
Nadia Hodge
Ruth Hodgkinson
Ann Hogan
Kilmeny Holleran
Angela Holohan
Maria Holovach
Kerenza Hood
Liz Hook
Liz Horn
Susan Houck
Deryn Howard

Helen Howard
Sarah Howard
Anita Howell
Christine Howes
Eleanor Howie
Alison Hueck
Becky Hughes
Derralynn Hughes
Peggy Hughes
Sarah Hughes
Clare Hulton
Janice Humphris
Mandy Hunsdale
Laura Hunter
For Ingrid
Helen Jackson
Kristina Jahnke-
    Frömmrich
Karolien Jaspers
Jaydeekay
Dawn Jehle
Claudia Jenkins
Sara Jewell
Joanna
Rebecca John
Marjorie Johns
Gregory Johns-Haist
Helen Jones
Lyn Jones
Melanie Jones
Philip Jones

Rachel N Jones
Rebecca Lewis Jones
Katya Jouravleva
Mary Jowitt
Judy Kamin
Helena Karaiskos
Susie Karrass
Hussain Kazi
Julie Keane
Paula Keane
Joanne Kearney
Liz Kebbell
Celina Kelley
Lisa Kelman
Helen Kembery
A Kennedy
Judy Kennedy
Emma Kennelly
Karen Kent
Liz Kentish
Adrienne Keown
Swetha Kerstjens
Sarah Keyes
Dan Kieran
Emily King
Karen King
Laura King
Kerri Kinghorn
Claire Kirby
Celia Kitzinger
Judith Kockelbergh

Sangeetha Kolluri
Claire Krickova
Anna Krolikowska
Kay Lake
Yvonne Lambdon
Mei-Ling Lancashire
Diana Lane
Katherine Latham
Kirsten Lavers
Geraldine Lavin
Stephanie Law
Julia Lawley
Barb Lawrie
Francois Le Goff
Jo Le Noury
Geraint Lee
Josephine Lee
Lesley
Lauren Lessiter
Kat Lewin-Harris
Anthony Lewis
Emma Lewis
Melissa Lewis
Sally Lewis
Beverley Lindsay
Joanna Lines
Bridget Little
Nikki Livingstone-
    Rothwell
Sara Liyanage
Rob Llewelyn

Maria Loftin
Jane Lomas
Berta Martin Lopez
Lisa Lougher
Clodagh Loughrey
Krista Lowe
Natalie Lower
Ciara Lyons
Sarah M
Carolyn MacCann
Ewan MacDermid
Colleen MacDonald
Laurie MacDougall
Gael MacLean
Catt★★ Makin
Philippa Manasseh
Anne Mannion
Kathryn Mannix
Marjon & Dimitris
Anna Marquiss
Gill Marriott
Helen Marshall
Roberta Marshall
Becky Martin
Trish Martin
Yazan Masannat
Steve Mash
Jane Mason
Sarah Massie
Jill Mayhew
Jane McCafferty

Catherine McClean
Maureen McCormack
Alison McCoubrey
Debbie Mccrossan
Lawrence McCrossan
Julie McCrossin
Beverley McGaughey
Patricia McGettigan
Carmel McGovern
Donna Mcharg
Fleur McIntosh
Cathy McIntyre
Tina McKenna
Scott McKenzie
Eleanor[8] McLaren
Gordon McLoughlin
Sharon McLoughlin
Rachel McMinnis
Dawn McMullan
Janet Mcnally
Wendelien McNicoll
Lesley McNulty
Sian Meades-Williams
Gail Medley
Katherine Mercer
Marcia Mercier
Andrea Merrill
Julie Mesny
Molly Miles
Cyndee Mitchell
Sally Mitchell

John Mitchinson
Foteini Mitsikosta
Liza Mitton
Paul Mizen
Jennifer Molina
Kerri Monk
Sue Morón-García
Beth Laura Morris
Craig Morrison
Henrietta Morrison
Jo Morrison
Emily Morter
Ania Motel
Beverley Mountain
Terry Mullan
Janice Mulley
Kim Mullins
Nancy Mulock
Aisling Mulvaney
Dr Catherine Munro
Anna Murphy
Tricia Murphy-Black
Sharon Murrin
Carlo Navato
Leigh-Anne Naylor
Sarah Naylor
Justine Neal
Nicola Neale
Julie Neu
Siobhán Neville
Mary Newman

Jo Newstead
Hayley Nicolaou
Elisabeth Nicoli
Juliet Nicolson
Pat Noto
Fiona O Dwyer
Clare O'Connell
Mary O'Dwyer
Clare O'Grady
Finola O'Neill
Dearbhaile O'Hare
Shelagh O'Riordan
Julie-anne Oakes
Kari Olsen-Porthouse
Barbara Olson
Lucy Olson
Tami Oren
Emma Osenton
Jennifer Ostroske
Sarah Parker
Elaine Parry
Pamela Parry
Fiona Partington
Rita Patel
Fiona Paterson
Lucy Pattullo
Paula
Laura Pawson
Taruna Peacock
Lily Pears
Kate Peet

Margaret Pelling
Guida Pereira
Josephine Perry
Nathan Pettitt
Gill Phillips
Roxy Philson
Lorna Pickard
Lorna Pirozzolo
Debbie Pitfield
Alison Pittard
Sarah Plant
Claire Platt
Justin Pollard
Theresa Porrett
Diane Potter
Jackie Pottle
Sarah Powell
Beth Preiss
Fiona Price
Jill Price
Laura Price
Nicola Prickett
Julie Prigg
Heidi Probst
Claire Pulford
Denise Purdon
Jan Purling
Heather Purnell
Samantha Purser
Bernadette Rae
Kaynath Rahman

Dee Rai
Laura Beatriz Calvo
    Ramos
Hazel Ratcliffe
Nicola Ratcliffe
Esther Rawlinson
Mar Ray
Natalie Rayers
Sarah Jane Relf
Ceri Renwick
Valerie Reynolds
Marianne Rial
Heather Rice
Kate Richmond
Deb Roberts
Dee Roberts
Geoffrey Roberts
Rachel Roberts
Susan Roberts
Elizabeth Robertson
Claire Robertson-
    Adams
Debbie Robinson
Ruth Robinson
Elaine Rodgers
Geraldine Rodgers OBE
Mary Rohan
Marianne Roper
Vicky Ropner
Victoria Rosengren
Rosie the Mermaid

Ashley Ross

Anna Round

Mechelle Rowe

Michelle Rowley

Lisa Rull

Jocelyn Ruparelia

Beverley Ruse

Tanya Russell

Ruth

Joanne Said

Pegah Salahshouri

Sally

Sammy

Amanda Sanderson

Juliana Santos

Melanie Saunders

Louise Schier

Clare Scott

Jo Scrutton

Kelly Shanahan

Laurence Shapiro

Pam Shepherd

Sue Shepherd

Keir Shiels

Hannah Short

Morag Shuaib

Stella Sibbit-Johnston

Melissa Siddorn

Emma Simmons

Emma Simons

Kate Simpson

Nikki Sinclair

Gillian Smellie

Alan C Smith

Alison Smith

Andrew Smith

B Smith

Becky Smith

Louise Smith

Naomi Smith

Ruth Smullen

Iain Snelling

Alexis Song

Barbara Southby

Lori Spadafore

Deborah Speed

Charlotte Squires

Nicola stanley

Val Stansfield

Angela Steen

Wendy Stephens

Lorraine Stevenson

Lynn Stevenson

Stephanie Stevenson

Judith Stoten

Rajko Strahinja

Laura Stranks

Carol Street

Catherine Strickland

Carolyn Stuart

Claire Stubbings

Paula Sugars

Carol Summerscales
Rebecca Sumnall
Charlotte Surguy
Susan
Claire Louise Sutton
Kathy Szczegolski
Anne Tagg
Emma Talbot
Fiona Talkington
Jayne Tansey-Patron
Robyn Tapp
Susan Tapp
Elizabeth Tapsell
Gail Tate
Vincent Taverner
Laura Taylor
Anna Thatcher
The Investment
  Association
Caroline Thomas
Lee Ann Thompson
Helen Tippett
Dawn Totty
Fay Tough
Towanda63
Margaret Townsend
Jo Tracy
Helen Treml
Ann Trewick
Sarah Tsopanis
Martine Tune

Allison Turner
Johanna Turner
Kate Turner
Pam Turner
Viviana Turturro
Jayne Tyler
Terri Tyndall
Dr. Asha Umrawsingh
Susanna Unsworth
Tiffany Upton
Rachel Upward
David Valls-Russell
Annemiek van der
  Heijden
Jeroen van Essen
Sarah Van Zoelen
John Vaughan
Zoe Veal
Elizabeth Venus
Jo W
Marie Wade
Janis Wagner
Lisa Wainwright MBE
Julie Wakeling
Deonne Wales
Jenny Walker
Thea Walker
Christine Wallace
Andrew Walling
Holly Wallis
Pete Wallroth

Clare Walsh
Margaret Walsh
Catherine Ward
Maura Warde
Jane Wareing
Claire Warnes
Karen Warren
Sue Warrington
Lindsey Waters
Ruth Waterton
Paula Watson
Lauren Watts
Lucy Watts
Tracy Waud
Briony Webber
Catriona Webster
Emma Weight
Jeremy Weinbren
Belinda Weir
Louise Welch
Catherine West
Tamsin Whalley
Sharon Wheeler
Jackie White

Michelle White
Wendy White
Liz Whyte
Ilana Widera
Chris Wilde
Gillian Wilkin
Jane Williams
Vicky Willmott-Stiles
Anna Wilson
Barbara Wilson
Jenny Wilson
Flora Winter
Frances Wiseman
Ellie Wishart
Nicola Withers
Theresa Witziers
Lynda Wixted
Claire Wood
Steven Wood
Alison Woods
Christie Wright
Kristin Wyman
Clare Wynn-Mackenzie
Chava Yanay

Thank yous

Thank you for sharing your extensive knowledge, insight and experience with such openness and generosity. You have a rare gift. Pat Noto

Thanks, Liz, for your courageous campaigning. When we finally meet, you can doodle on this dedication in my precious copy of your book. Much love, Kathryn Mannix xx

Thanks, Liz, for telling this story in your own words. It will touch so many lives in such a positive way. Sarah Massie

Thank you, Liz O'Riordan, and the countless women who have walked this path before me. Together, they strengthened me with their love and courage, whilst I searched for my own. Pam Chappell

For all of the men and women who have been touched by cancer. Stay strong! Lauren Bishop

One of my best friends is fighting bravely against breast cancer, her optimism is an inspiration to me. I wish she will find strength and hope from this book. Francis Xi

Thank you to the NHS and all the charities for their support. Liberty Godwin

Thank you so much for everything you have taught me about breast cancer and the support it gave me for my precious time with my sister. Jane Dickson

Thank you for telling your story here and for sharing a part of your life with so many of us. Anne Cheng

You have helped me in my darkest hours. Sue Hall x

Thank you, Liz, for all you do to give us women with breast cancer a voice. Lorna Pirozzolo

Thank you, Liz, for all your support for https://www. frommetoyouletters.co.uk. Liz Kentish

The raw honesty of the impact of the diagnosis and the consequences for your career and how you dealt with the highs and lows will resonate with others. So candid. Julie Mesny

A sign that us women can do anything and everything we want to! Lauren Ayms X

Thank you for your insightful no-nonsense advice. It has been, and continues to be, invaluable. Wishing you every success with this book, I can't wait to read it! Elaine Rodgers

Thank you for inspiring me to take on whatever challenges life throws my way, and proving to myself I really can be one of healthcare's kick-ass fabulous women! Christine H